Foundational Economy

Manchester University Press

The *Manchester Capitalism* book series

GENERAL EDITORS: JULIE FROUD AND KAREL WILLIAMS

Manchester Capitalism is a series of books which follows the trail of money and power across the systems of our failing capitalism. The books make powerful interventions about who gets what and why in a research based and solidly argued way that is accessible for the concerned citizen. They go beyond critique of neo liberalism and its satellite knowledges to re-frame our problems and offer solutions about what is to be done.

Manchester was the city of Engels and Free Trade where the twin philosophies of collectivism and free market liberalism were elaborated. It is now the home of this venture in radical thinking that challenges self-serving elites. We see the provincial radicalism rooted here as the ideal place from which to cast a cold light on the big issues of economic renewal, financial reform and political mobilisation.

Already published:

The end of the experiment: From competition to the foundational economy

What a waste: Outsourcing and how it goes wrong

Licensed larceny: Infrastructure, financial extraction and the global South

The econocracy: The perils of leaving economics to the experts

Reckless opportunists: Elites at the end of the establishment

Forthcoming:

Safe as houses: Private greed, political negligence and housing policy after Grenfell

Systems city: A new politics of provision for an urbanized planet

Praise for *Foundational Economy*

'A compelling counter-project against neoliberalism: restoring the collective foundations of everyday life'
Wolfgang Streeck, Max Planck Institute for the Study of Societies, Germany

'This is an interesting and important contribution to the economic debates going on today. It underlines the centrality of collectivism and universalism as pillars of a decent society, as well as asking searching questions about the kind of solutions we need to the economic problems of our age.'
John McDonnell, Shadow Chancellor of the Exchequer

'Something has gone very wrong with the British economy. Investment and growth is poor and the proceeds are not fairly shared. Pay is unequal and stagnating for the majority. Too many people are trapped in insecure, low-paid and zero hours work. Outsourcing giants make a killing extracting value from our public services. And affordable housing remains a distant dream, especially for young families. This is the everyday reality that working people face and *Foundational Economy* sets out a razor sharp analysis of the reasons why. But, more importantly, it delivers practical proposals for change. A smart and dynamic state at a national and local level, democratisation of our communities and workplaces, investment in public services - and those parts of our economy that most people depend on and where most people earn their living. This agenda poses big challenges for policy makers, politicians and civil society alike. But they must be met if we are to have an intelligent industrial policy for economic justice and twenty-first-century public services that meet the needs of every community across the UK. Doing more of the same is not an option. *Foundational Economy* provides a springboard for the new deal working people need.'
Frances O'Grady, General Secretary, Trades Union Congress

'An essential attempt to transform how we think about economics, a searing critique of where we've gone wrong, and a powerful call for a renewed "provincial radicalism". This is a key contribution towards building a more equal and democratic economy and to reconnecting economics and politics with the everyday lives of communities across Britain.'

Rachel Reeves MP, Labour Party politician, economist and chair of the Business, Energy and Industrial Strategy Committee

'This fascinating book, *Foundational Economy*, can be seen as a contribution to the debate about measuring, understanding and, ultimately, reshaping economic systems. More than that, it is a critique of existing custom and practice when measuring, understanding and shaping the economy. This critique is as foundational as the book's title. We are some way short of a well-defined and widely-agreed set of new weights and measures for the economy. And we are a long way short of knowing which policy tools best deliver the private and collective goods society needs to flourish. This book tackles head-on some of those big questions about the economy. It also begins the process of providing answers. As in the natural sciences, as an approach I think this offers hope for societal, as well as scientific, advance.'

Andy Haldane, Chief Economist, Bank of England

'There is now a widespread and growing view that the UK economy has ceased to work effectively for ordinary people. This original and challenging book sets out a compelling argument for why this is happening. You do not have to sign up to every individual point made in the book to recognise the power of the overall argument. At the heart of the book is the idea of the 'foundational economy', its rise in the municipal era, its fall in the neo-liberal era and how it might be renewed again. The term foundational may not be in everyday use but what it describes represents the essential fabric of our lives – the essential infrastructure of energy, water and transport, and the essential services of education,

health and care. These are distinguished by being essentially collective goods. They cannot simply be 'bought' by an individual but must be decided by society as a whole. For the last 30 or so years, it has been the accepted wisdom of many politicians and policy makers that these services are best enabled publicly but delivered privately. The book provides a robust challenge to this view. Those looking to find individual policy solutions in this book will be disappointed. It is much more about changing the way we think about economics and society. But is does contain a message of hope in some pretty challenging times. Recommended reading lists for civil servants are quite a common occurrence at Christmas time. This book deserves to be on those lists.'
Lord Bob Kerslake, Head of the UK Civil Service, 2011-14

'For decades economic policy has been done to people and not with and by them. It has not for the most part focused on the sectors of the economy that matter to people every day or on the communities that most need to benefit. The foundational economy approach represents a move away from grand industrial projects and the unaccountable power of neo-classical economics. In a world of falling living standards, wellbeing in reverse gear, enormous wealth inequality and urgent environmental crises, it is an approach whose time has come.'
Andrew Pendleton, Director of Policy and Advocacy at the New Economics Foundation

'In the honourable tradition of provincial radicalism, the Foundational Economy Collective open new horizons for social, economic and political renewal with their provocative and yet practical proposals for reconstructing everyday economies. This is not the time for incremental tinkering with the status quo, nor critique solely for its own sake. Instead, *Foundational Economy* delivers an arresting and imaginative manifesto for rebuilding our communities from the ground up. Founded on a political economy of hope, not despair, this approach is

radical in all of the best senses of the word: it cuts to the root of wicked problems, rethinking from first principles; it steadfastly refuses to be cowed or constrained by stale orthodoxies; and it illuminates an alternative pathway, guided by the principles of inclusive citizenship, social innovation, ethical investment, and progressive political renewal. This is a book that is sure to change some minds, and maybe even the future.'
Jamie Peck, University of British Columbia, Canada

'Read this book if you want to understand why the NHS is not funded through taxes raised from the private sector; if you want to know why our children will not be mostly employed in 'high tech' industry in future (and cannot be); why the welfare state was a good protection racket; why British privatised rail companies lie so much about their 'greatness'; why care homes are so badly run at such great private profit by 'entrepreneurs'; and how those who rob us so often claim a defence of 'diminished responsibility' for their acts of great harm. All that is in just the first two chapters of *Foundational Economy*. The collective that produced this book of wonders deserves to be warmly congratulated on producing such a clear explanation of, amongst so much else, how "the British and Americans led the way to a new kind of rentier capitalism." And what now to do about it – in a way that cannot be as easily extinguished as radical politics in the recent past has been.'
Danny Dorling, University of Oxford

'A dedicated group of scholars across a broad range of disciplines at Manchester University have long led the way in detailing and analysing what the late Michael Moran, one of the foremost among them, identified as the "financial services revolution" at the root of the transformation of public policy into the handmaiden of privatisation and marketisation. This new book, perfectly timed to coincide with the growing populist disgust with what they call "a generation of failure to make

the market work", concentrates on penetrating the fog currently generated by all the talk across the political spectrum about the importance of investment in infrastructure. Brilliantly conceiving and concisely explaining in historical and comparative perspective the social and moral basis of "foundational" goods and services, this book is essential reading for all concerned to escape the predations of financial engineering and bring the "everyday infrastructure of civilised life" into the public domain under democratic control.'
Leo Panitch, York University, Canada and editor of *The Socialist Register*

'Citizens have rights to basic services because their public provision underpins capacities and capabilities for all. This inspirational reformulation of the Foundational Economy explains why we need to stop wrecking our public services in Europe and start refashioning their future in the twenty-first century. It is not enough to claim that the Foundation Economy is a moral enterprise and the authors lay out new directions for social innovation enabling us to reinvent both our political practice and the world we hope for.'
Henrietta L. Moore, Director of the UCL Global Prosperity Institute

'*Foundational Economy* outlines the need for collective provision of the essential services which are the social infrastructure of everyday life. Its arguments and strategies are a vital contribution to the debate across Europe about renewing progressive economic policies. The book provides meticulous historical evidence as to the way collective provision was eroded under neoliberalism, and evidence-based ideas for what states, collectives and individuals can do. It is a major contribution to the debate about how we can actively shape our post capitalist future.'
Paul Mason, journalist and author of *PostCapitalism: A Guide to Our Future*

'So much of the writing since the crash has been glib optimism, smartly-packaged gobbets of wishful thinking. This book is nothing of the sort. It is a draught of cold realism. Britain isn't going back to some mythical golden age nor will it catapult into some jetpack future, so it's time to face ugly facts and think harder about how to create the society and economy we want. The authors are engaged academics and they bring analytical hard-headedness, a fresh political imagination – and a welcome outsider chippiness. This is the kind of economics that never makes it onto the City pages, the sort of politics that rarely gets into newspaper columns. Read it.'
Aditya Chakrabortty, Senior Economics Commentator, *The Guardian*

'The rise in economic, social and recognition inequalities and the correlated authoritarian dynamic are not the result of unavoidable system changes, but of policy choices and a change in both the balance of power and common sense. The research team which has launched the Foundational Economy project now addresses these issues by forcefully outlining a reversal of policymaking so that citizen's capabilities, substantive freedom and social consumption regain centre stage. A welcome contribution to the urgent rethinking of economics and politics.'
Fabrizio Barca, previously Divisional Head of Research at the Bank of Italy, special adviser to the EU Commissioner responsible for regional policy and Italian Minister of Territorial Cohesion (2011-13)

'Since 1988, Barcelona has developed five strategic plans, all of them having "business friendly" postulates as their basis. When a year ago the new team in charge of the future metropolitan strategy decided to place five basic elements for life (air, water, food, energy and housing) as the core elements for that strategy, we did not know a word about the proposal of the Foundational Economy. Now that we have had the opportunity to read this inspiring book, we not only consider our vision strengthened, but we also have the elements to more solidly support it and even reinforce it, incorporating some of the valuable insights that the authors provide. A must-read for all of us who are committed to improve wellbeing in our cities and our society in general.'

Oriol Estela Barnet, General Co-ordinator of PEMB, The Office for Strategic Planning of the City and Metropolitan Area of Barcelona; previously Head of the Office for Local Economic Development (2012–16)

'In this book the authors present an innovative and creative account of economic development, one driven by the need to preserve our "Foundational Economy" in Europe. To do this the authors convincingly make the case that Europe's foundational economy is a significant driver of social not simply individual market driven consumption. The distinctive primary role of public policy is about how experimentation, at a local level, can be directed to help secure the continuity of basic foundational services upon which Europe's citizens depend and need to flourish.'

Theodor Dumitru Stolojan, European People's Party group (Christian Democrats), Chairman of the IFRS Permanente team of the European Parliament, previously Prime Minister of Romania 1991–92 and presidential candidate 2000 and 2004)

'In *Foundational Economy* we are presented with an alternative and refreshing view of social policy. The innovative argument presented by this Europe-wide collective group of authors is that the primary role of public policy should be re-aligned towards promoting the 'Foundational Economy'. These foundational activities are often overlooked and, to a significant extent, taken for granted. But they should not be overlooked because these activities generate social consumption upon which all citizens across Europe depend for our collective welfare, household employment and general well-being.'

Eva Kaili MEP, Group of the Progressive Alliance of Socialists and Democrats in the European Parliament

Foundational Economy

The infrastructure of everyday life

Foundational Economy Collective

*Davide Arcidiacono, Filippo Barbera, Andrew Bowman,
John Buchanan, Sandro Busso, Joselle Dagnes, Joe Earle,
Ewald Engelen, Peter Folkman, Julie Froud, Colin Haslam,
Sukhdev Johal, Ian Rees Jones, Dario Minervini,
Mick Moran, Fabio Mostaccio, Gabriella Pauli,
Leonhard Plank, Angelo Salento, Ferdinando Spina,
Nick Tsitsianis, Karel Williams*

Manchester University Press

Published by Manchester University Press
Altrincham Street, Manchester M1 7JA

www.manchesteruniversitypress.co.uk

British Library Cataloguing-in-Publication Data
A catalogue record for this book is available from the British
Library

ISBN   978 1 5261 3399 1   hardback
ISBN   978 1 5261 3400 4   paperback

First published 2018

Typeset
by Toppan Best-set Premedia Limited
Printed in Great Britain
by Bell & Bain Ltd, Glasgow

Contents

List of exhibits

Foreword by Colin Crouch

All who have spent much of their lives writing would hope that their final contribution would be something profound, leaving behind an important message, well stated. That *Foundational Economy* achieves this for Mick Moran is the only consolation of his death, which occurred barely five weeks after he had asked me to write this Foreword. Mick was still at the peak of his creative and innovative powers and this book is the result of his driving role in a fruitful collaboration with his other authors and a larger collective group.

Joseph Schumpeter described one form of innovation as the bringing together of things previously unassociated. *Foundational Economy* is a book which does this for some central themes: the need for and neglect of infrastructure and problems arising in the outsourcing of its provision and the privileging of financial services over other activities; the neglect of the basic in the search for the dazzlingly new; the rights and duties of citizenship; Amartya Sen and Martha Nussbaum's concept of capabilities; regional and urban industrial policy. These are all brought together within the idea of the foundational economy: those goods, services and other forms of provision that are necessary for the good life to be enjoyed by as many people as possible.

Paradoxically, what is basic and foundational is always likely to be taken for granted, and as a result neglected, until we notice that much of it has slipped away, and become very difficult to replace. The foundational is not often at the cutting edge and therefore lacks both glamour and novelty. Announce at a smart party that you work for an internet company and the crowd will gather round; say that you are a water engineer and few people will want to know more – unless you are with a private water firm that has produced leaking water mains because it pursued dividends at the expense of maintaining its infrastructure. You are unlikely to announce that you are a care worker for the elderly, because care workers are unlikely to appear at smart parties. To this problem of the basic of being taken for granted, recent times have added further elements. Three of the extraordinary ideological triumphs of neoliberal ideas have been widespread acceptance: first, that financial transactions are the most valuable kind of economic activity, and as many other activities as possible should develop their financial possibilities; second, that the collective is always inferior to the individual, and should if possible be redefined in terms of the latter; third, that no goods or services are more important than others and therefore all can be traded in one market.

The neglect of infrastructure and other elements of the foundational economy follows fairly logically from these three postulates. The provision of public services is outsourced to firms, whose major project is using these services for conversion into financial assets. The consequent neglect of the substantive service is not important as, being a collective good, it was not important; and so-called public services must take their chance with all other goods and services for funding. A further consequence is a redefinition of what is meant by citizenship. Historically associated with membership of a collectivity and the stream of rights and duties flowing from that, it has often come to mean the rights of an individual almost against the community, as in rights not to be disturbed, to be regulated, to pay taxes. One recalls the 1991 Citizen's Charter of the British prime minister John Major, which set out the expectations people might have of their public services. Announced in speeches before it appeared in written form, many expected it to be 'Citizens", but no, the government very firmly chose to address citizens as individuals rather than as people sharing something in common.

This triumph has however been far from total. Very few outside the neoliberal ideological community itself have accepted that money spent on health or education is morally indistinguishable from that spent on leisure activities, or that financial transactions constitute the highest form of economic activity. And sometimes even the staunchest defenders of individualism – including prominently Margaret Thatcher herself – would respond to demands for rights to some kind of public service with the entirely appropriate rejoinder that rights imply duties. It is easy to neglect and even disparage the foundational, far more difficult to dispose of it.

Most human beings will accept that they are dependent on others in various ways for mere survival, let alone flourishing and enjoying a good life, and that this dependency cannot be reduced to market transactions alone. What they may resent are the obligations that this acceptance requires. The motorist who celebrates the individual freedom that driving gives him might recall that this freedom is dependent on the provision of public roads only when he bursts a tyre on an unrepaired pothole. And even then he might continue voting for politicians who promise lower local taxes, forgetting that it was that which led to the pothole being unrepaired.

Some elements of a collective life are necessary for almost everything else we want to do, whether together or alone; and these elements are often in themselves unglamorous and without high added value in strict economic theory terms. As the authors freely admit, the list of these elements is not fixed for all time and all places. Some are – water for example. Others come and go with economic advance and changing cultural preferences. Sen and Nussbaum's capabilities provide an excellent place to start, though, as this book argues, the list (though it is not really as crude as a series of listed items) requires permanent democratic debate and adjustment. These elements, being basic, are part of our rights, our entitlement as citizens of a political community, and therefore need to be available even if we cannot afford them in the market or if there are inadequate incentives for firms to provide them within the market. In exchange we have a reciprocal duty to accept the same rights for our fellow citizens, be willing to pay for their provision through taxes, and perhaps to campaign and work for continuity and improvement of provision.

The importance of the urban

Foundational Economy makes interesting use of T. H. Green, the liberal collectivist, sometimes known as an English Hegelian, who wrote of the reciprocal relationship of the individual and society and the importance of public works, including the sustaining of urban infrastructure. Urban life has long been a principal reminder of our collective interdependence. The medieval cities of Europe were often sites of experiments in forms of governance, basic measures of hygiene, and the construction of shared spaces. The nineteenth century industrial city massively intensified the problems raised by large numbers of persons living in close proximity, while science was revealing more of the health and safety requirements of such a life. This was where Green and many other social reformers of the period took their inspiration for further explorations of the role of collectivity and citizenship.

Today we know even more about the needs of urban structures if they are to support thriving economies and worthwhile lives. Their economies need not only road and rail networks and educational facilities but also elements of community that can enable local producers to benefit from each other's knowledge and experience even when they remain competitors. Cities need parks, local cultural icons, features that enable their residents to feel a sense of proud belonging and purpose. The market will provide some of these things, but not all, and there is a strong tendency for the market to slip towards already privileged and established locations, leaving many areas behind with little beyond warehouses and call centres. Indeed, public policy has often followed the market, intensifying problems of geographical inequality. In Britain large sums of public money are spent to sustain London and the South East as economic powerhouses and attractive places in which to live, while proposals to revive the declining towns of the North and Midlands are met with criticism and scepticism. Capitals and other leading cities and regions might attract and then gain further from market activities, but it was rarely the market that provided the foundations of their success. Capital cities in particular have been public projects, often being built up over centuries to be worthy seats of monarchs and later of modern governments.

We are today in need of a new burst of foundational energy around urban and regional development. Our equivalents of the city fathers of thirteenth century Siena or of nineteenth century urban social reformers certainly exist and contribute actively to debate. Their proposals are not necessarily for glamorous high-tech projects, just the basic elements that make a town a good place to be. But they are largely being ignored. The very wealthy increasingly live in gated communities where they enjoy private public provision behind the protection of security guards and CCTV cameras. They speed from one privileged private location to another in limousines with tinted windows, rarely entering a public street in any other way. Their way of life requires an enormous infrastructure, but it is not shared by the rest of the city.

People living in neglected regions believe that they can do little to challenge the power structure that is doing so little for them. Increasing numbers of them are therefore venting their anger on weak, easily identifiable targets, mainly immigrants and ethnic minorities. Or they are gaining a vicarious association with national elites by being hostile to foreigners in general. It is remarkable how the recent waves of xenophobia in many countries have not been shared by the populations of capitals and other cities whose residents can feel proud of the present and confident about the future. The residents of Budapest have largely resisted the massive xenophobic wave in Hungary; those of Vienna, Salzburg and Graz, or of Milan and Rome, the smaller waves in Austria and Italy. Only minorities of Londoners, Mancunians and Liverpudlians voted for Brexit. Californians largely rejected the appeal of Donald Trump.

The foundational and the state

For figures like T. H. Green the idea of liberal collectivism was not an oxymoron. The development of the individual was a condition for the development of the collective, and vice versa. The relationship was entirely reciprocal. The same is true of Amartya Sen and countless other lesser figures who think about these things. But for many the tension between the collective and the individual who is central to the liberal world view is unbridgeable. For this we can partly blame contemporary economic and political theory, which have placed the totally self-oriented, rationally choosing, context-free individual at the heart of their models of human life. In this they are so different from the own predecessors, such as Adam Smith or Thomas Hobbes. But there is something else more challenging here.

Green and others could take concepts from Hegel, in particular the importance to the individual of being part of a collective represented largely by the state, without the shadows that the twentieth century was to cast over them. Both Nazism and Soviet socialism drew on Hegel as one, though only one, of the sources of their images of the individual as a petty and worthless thing in the face of the might of the collective as embodied in a state. And their states became increasingly violent and tyrannical.

Of course, it does not have to be like that. Decades of democratic and liberal governments in the Nordic countries and shorter episodes in the UK, Germany, France and elsewhere have shown that an appreciation of the importance of the state, deriving from socialist ideas, does not need in any way to be hostile to free individual expression, diversity, toleration of difference. Nevertheless, it would be folly to ignore the impact that the fall of the Soviet system after 1990 has had for collectivist political projects. We already knew about the dictatorships, the Gulag, the Stasi. But we then learned that state socialism had also neglected the very things it might have been expected to offer in part compensation. Urban infrastructure outside a few prestige cities was a disaster. Pollution and environmental damage were very high. The Soviet experience has given statist collectivism a very bad name.

One can deal with this by pointing again to the north-west European experience. But *Foundational Economy* goes a considerable step further. In this book, the idea of the collective is not synonymous with the state. Theoretically this is straightforward enough; the two concepts are different in structure. In practice however many political thinkers perform a couple of manoeuvres to end up with the state being de facto the most practical form that the collective can take, at least in anything beyond a small community. What is important is that the actors or providers engaged in the foundational economy work to an ethic that goes beyond the hypothetical individual who is the end point of action in orthodox economic theory. This goal can be achieved in a number of ways, including direct state action, but also regulation and ultimately dependence on the vigilance and concern of citizens. Society is therefore shot through with responsibility for the foundational. Private firms engaged in the provision of these services need to be subject to these ethical constraints, rather than to the goal of financial maximisation embodied in contemporary doctrines of corporate governance.

Despite their differences, classical economists and socialist theorists are likely to agree on keeping the private sector and the state very separate. The challenge that Moran and his co-authors pose to this customary way of thinking marks a further important contribution of this book. They have pointed the way to so many constructive new approaches. We must hope that many others will follow them down that path; it is sad that Mick will no longer be here to help us on the way.

Colin Crouch

Acknowledgements

Producing this book dramatises an important truth: almost all the important things that we do in life are only possible when we work collectively, and many of the best things come from voluntary association without financial motive. That, in turn, demands qualities of independence, generosity and tolerance, which are not always in abundant supply in the increasingly individualised, performance-oriented culture of our universities. It also requires a broader network outside academia that provides encouraging support and constructive criticism.

The division of labour within the collective is as explained in Chapter 1. This book was directly authored by a gang of five: the text was drafted and redrafted by Mick Moran and Karel Williams, who were closely advised and prompted on structural decisions, shaping of the argument and exhibits for each chapter by Julie Froud, Sukhdev Johal and Angelo Salento. Other members of the foundational collective contributed notes and drafts for chapters within book plans, which were hammered out by the whole group in three seminar meetings in Turin, London and Lecce. We are grateful to the Universities of Turin and Salento, and Queen Mary University of London for their financial support for those meetings.

The stock of ideas is collective and the creativity and scope of the book's argument owes everything to the group. But behind the members of the Foundational Economy Collective are many academic friends and professional colleagues who have unstintingly given their time and energy to support our work over several years, and this book project over the past eighteen months. Beyond these professional obligations we should also explain how this book is grounded in present-day provincial radicalism, honours the families and communities we come from and is dedicated to the medics and paramedics of three European cities.

Our publishers at Manchester University Press, under Simon Ross, remain dedicated to the best traditions of University publishing – in other words, to the increasingly difficult job of reconciling commercial viability with producing imaginative work in the public interest. We owe a particular debt to two people at the Press: to MUP's editorial director, Emma Brennan, who initiated and has always supported the *Manchester Capitalism* series of short, radical books; and to MUP's commissioning editor, Tom Dark, who has coached us and his other authors with a combination of positive enthusiasm and firm guidance about what will or will not work.

Critical academic friends have shaped our ideas in many ways. Their generosity is all the more remarkable because they do not always agree with our often clumsy formulations in these pages. John Law did not join us in this project but played an important role in the initial development of the foundational economy concept; more recently, Kevin Morgan has gone well beyond the call of duty or friendship in his engagement with our ideas, including detailed comments on our drafts for this book. More specifically, we should thank Dan Coffey, from whom we received the notion of the 'overlooked economy', which is important to the shape of our argument.

Through the Welsh connection, practitioners have also been hugely important in the dialogue which has developed our ideas. Iestyn Davies and Rachel Bowen, then at the Federation of Small Businesses Wales, and Debbie Green of Coastal Housing, separately commissioned us to write two public interest reports. Welsh Assembly members from Labour and Plaid Cymru have then challenged us to articulate alternative policies while they pressed the case for Welsh Government engagement with foundational sectors. Diolch i Aelodau'r Cynulliad: Hefin David, Vikki Howells, Jeremy Miles, Adam Price and Lee Waters.

This book is grounded in provincial radicalism in a different way through lived connections with the families and communities we come from and all our migrant pasts. We remember the parent who wired the house for electricity in the 1950s, and the grandparent photographed against the outside flush toilet which was, in the early 1930s, the first in the street. We have all benefited from social and geographic mobility. And, for us, social mobility and historical time is not about leaving people and places behind but about gaining the perspective to honour what was valuable in our collective past and can now be renewed through our intellectual and political work.

And if that work is challenging, this is anything but a lost cause when so much public service today still delivers on the foundational values and priorities that concern us in this book. It was planned and drafted when we were dealing with breast cancer at our publisher, lymphoma in the gang of five and ovarian cancer in the partner of a collective member. Our readers will therefore understand why this book is gratefully dedicated to the medics and paramedics who treated our friends and serve all the citizens of London, Manchester and Vienna.

But some things are beyond medical intervention. Suddenly and completely unexpectedly, Mick Moran died of one massive heart attack three months after the manuscript of this book been delivered to the publisher and when we had just started to talk about our next writing projects. His family were grief stricken and the little gang of authors, who had worked with Mick on four joint-authored books, were disconsolate. In remembering Mick publicly, we do now want to record that his was a foundational story of lived experience and values.

Mick was against sentimentalizing the past and always insisted there never was a golden age. But his own life shows what a child of poor migrants could achieve, in that brief period up to the late 1970s when many of the problems of high-income capitalist societies seemed amenable to economic management and social intervention. His academic life is the story of what publicly funded education did for a bright Irish Brummie boy who went to university on a full maintenance grant before contributing so much for fifty years to non-state collectivism through his church, community, discipline and university.

Through the Thatcher and Blair years, Mick had always retained a certain residual respect for our governing elites. The 2008 financial crisis was an epiphany because it convinced him that the officer class in business and politics did not know what it was doing. He went on to write disruptive books with us, starting with a 2011 study of the great financial crisis, *After the Great Complacence*, which uniquely combines economic and political analysis.

He was afterwards a driving force in developing foundational thinking and *Foundational Economy* is now the last, most radical and well-wrought of those jointly authored books. He worked on it fiercely, with intellectual imagination and political hope to make the world a better place. Appropriately, this book is about renewing the citizens' right to collective goods and services, whose provision in 1960s Britain gave Mick his start in academic life.

What readers make of this book depends on what they bring to it and we trust that most will recognise a constructive attempt to sketch a new foundational agenda where there is room for many different actors and ideologies in alliance. Our scepticism about much of what is done as economics combines with a commitment to critical social science knowledges; our concern for citizens and participation does not imply disrespect for expertise and planning.

To underscore these points, we asked a radical political scientist and a free-thinking economic policymaker to respond to our argument. Hence the foreword by Colin Crouch and the afterword by Andy Haldane which give you very different responses to our book. The rest is up to you.

The members of the Foundational Economy collective are: Davide Arcidiacono, Filippo Barbera, Andrew Bowman, John Buchanan, Sandro Busso, Joselle Dagnes, Joe Earle, Ewald Engelen, Peter Folkman, Julie Froud, Colin Haslam, Sukhdev Johal, Ian Rees Jones, Dario Minervini, Mick Moran, Fabio Mostaccio, Gabriella Pauli, Leonhard Plank, Angelo Salento, Ferdinando Spina, Nick Tsitsianis, Karel Williams.

This book is being published in English, German and Italian by Manchester University Press, Suhrkamp and Einaudi.

Our ongoing work can be tracked through the foundationaleconomy.com website.

Abbreviations and glossary

BIEN	Basic Income Earth Network
CAFOD	Catholic Agency For Overseas Development
EU 28	The 28 member states of the EU
FSI	Ferrovie dello Stato Italiane (Italian rail holding company)
G7	A group of seven countries (Canada, France, Germany, Italy, Japan, the UK and the US) which meet periodically to discuss economic and finance issues
G20	A group of 19 countries plus the EU whose governments and central banks meet periodically and work together on some policies
GDP	Gross Domestic Product. GDP is measured as the value of all the finished goods and services produced in a particular place (e.g. a region or nation) during a specific period (e.g. a year)
GM	Greater Manchester. The Greater Manchester city region covers ten boroughs – Bolton, Bury, Manchester, Oldham, Rochdale, Salford, Stockport, Tameside, Trafford, Wigan
GMCA	Greater Manchester Combined Authority. A regional governing body covering the ten boroughs that comprise the Greater Manchester city region
GNI	Gross National Income. GNI is the total domestic and foreign output claimed by residents of a country:

	calculated as GDP, plus factor incomes earned by foreign residents, minus income earned in the domestic economy by non-residents
GVA	gross value added. GVA is measured as the value of goods and services produced (in a particular place during a specific period), minus the cost of all inputs and raw materials that are directly attributable to its production
KIBS	knowledge-intensive business services
MIT	Massachusetts Institute of Technology
NACE	The EU system for statistical classification of economic activities (industries). NACE is from the French term *nomenclature statistique des activités économiques dans la Communauté Européenne*
NHS	National Health Service
OECD	Organisation for Economic Co-operation and Development
ONS	Office for National Statistics (the UK national statistics agency)
ROCE	return on capital employed (calculated as the profit divided by all the long-term capital in the business – debt and equity). The ROCE is presented as a percentage and shows the amount of profit per unit (e.g. pound) of long-term capital invested in the business
SIC	standard industry classification. A system of industry or economic activity classification for statistical collection
SME	small and medium-sized enterprise
UCL	University College London

1 Introduction: foundational matters

To be truly radical is to make hope possible, rather than despair convincing. (Raymond Williams, *Resources of Hope*, 1989, p. 118)

This book aims to change established ways of thinking about economy, society and politics. It argues that the well-being of Europe's citizens depends less on individual consumption and more on their social consumption of essential goods and services – from water and retail banking, to schools and care homes – in what we call *the foundational economy*. Individual consumption depends on market income, while foundational consumption depends on infrastructure and delivery systems of networks and branches, which are neither created nor renewed automatically, even as incomes increase. The distinctive, primary role of public policy should therefore be to secure the supply of basic services for all citizens. If the aim is citizen well-being and flourishing for the many not the few, then European politics at regional, national and EU level needs to be refocused on foundational consumption and securing universal minimum access and quality.

Since the 1980s, the public policy debate has been about whether the state should continue to deliver many of these foundational services. This is an important debate because, as we will argue, privatisation and outsourcing of foundational services is damaging. But we have lost sight of the fundamental issue about the unique value of foundational consumption and how it is not guaranteed by high or rising individual incomes. This last point was very clearly understood by earlier generations of socialists and liberal collectivists. For R.H. Tawney in 1931, piped water and sanitation had transformed big cities and demonstrated society's 'collective provision for needs which no ordinary individual, even if he works overtime all his life, can provide himself' (pp. 134–5). J.K. Galbraith in 1958 restated the problem as one of 'social balance': individual incomes were increasing in the US, while schools and public transport decayed and air pollution increased, so that 'the discussion of this public poverty was matched by the stories of ever increasing private opulence' (p. 187).

What high-income countries have done for the past fifty years is feed this imbalance through promoting a narrow concept of economic policy which incidentally embeds a top-down setting of priorities. Public policy is something done by technical and political elites to and for ordinary citizens, often under the guise of governance arrangements that emphasise individual choice and responsibility. Since the Second World War, 'the economy' has been managed (by fiscal or monetary policy) for growth of Gross Domestic Product (GDP), with welfare primarily distributed through individual consumption based on wages. And since the late 1970s there has also been a presupposition in favour of competition and markets through structural reform which aims to make labour markets more flexible and introduces large-scale privatisation and outsourcing. In all of this, foundational services and the infrastructures that enable them to be provided are subordinate. It is assumed that income support must not interfere with work incentives, education should create workforce skills and health services are to be funded from taxes on incomes, even as tax rates are being cut and growth is increasingly hard to find.

Public policy since the 1980s has pursued the ideal of a market economy for the twenty-first century and, by the 2010s, has ended up recreating a predatory capitalism with income and wealth inequalities at nineteenth-century levels. What is more, stalled income growth across Europe threatens the political franchises of centrist parties of government. This economic outcome is dissected acutely by Thomas Piketty in his book *Capital in the Twenty-First Century*. But Piketty's diagnosis is much stronger than his prescription – redistribution through a global wealth tax – which he accepts is 'utopian'. We try to avoid utopianism by updating the old arguments about foundational services for new times in four chapters which present description, analysis and proposals for what is to be done. Against a depressing European background, our aim is to make hope possible.

Chapter 2 describes the foundational economy and presents a brief history which provides essential context for all subsequent argument. The foundational concept focuses attention on the goods and services which are the social and material infrastructure of civilised life because they provide daily essentials for all households. These include material services through pipes and cables, networks and branches distributing water, electricity, banking services and food; and the providential services of education, and health and social care, as well as income maintenance. These are welfare-critical activities for all households in the sense that limited access has a significant effect on the welfare of households and social economic opportunity for citizens. The foundational economy is also important as a source of employment: right across Europe, 40% of the workforce is in these 'sheltered' activities – meaning that they are generally not subject to the pressures of international competition. Physical access to and pricing of foundational services depend on public or private investment decisions about networks and branches, plus political choices about operating subsidies from tax revenue. Any individual can buy a computer, but high-speed internet access depends on the material infrastructure telecoms companies provide.

A brief history of the foundational economy since 1850 highlights two heroic periods of construction, followed, since

1970, by a very different phase of gradual degradation. In the first phase after 1850, municipalities led in providing gas, water and sanitation, which transformed life quality and added decades to life expectancy in Europe's great cities. In the second phase, after 1945, the central state, which had already taken the leading role in organising income maintenance through social insurance, now nationalised much of the patchwork provision of material services. But it turned out that what the central state had created, it could also take away. After the early 1980s, at a variable pace in different European countries, central state power has taken a destructive turn through privatisation, outsourcing and service cuts.

Chapters 3 and 4 of the book move from description to analysis – a necessary prelude to any discussion of policy responses. Chapter 3 presents a 'follow-the-money' analysis of how and why privatisation and outsourcing disappoint and damage, while Chapter 4 presents an argument about the rights and duties of citizenship.

If post-1980 privatisation and outsourcing have ended in disappointment, this relates partly to specific issues about irrelevant regulation in privatised utilities and crisis-prone conglomerates in outsourcing. Regulation of privatised utilities was dominated by economists focused on policing prices and investment and concerned to promote competition. At the same time, managers and fund investors were engineering cash extraction so that in the privatised UK water industry, for instance, the regulator allowed all the profits to be distributed as dividends, while investment was financed by adding debt. If we turn to outsourcing of public services in areas like health, justice or welfare administration, this is complicated by the involvement of large conglomerates, under financial market pressure for growth. In search of revenue growth, they move into new activity areas until their luck runs out, typically on contracts they do not understand.

More fundamentally, Chapter 3 argues, that there is a general problem about new entrants with high expectations of return and unsuitable business models. The foundational economy (public or private) had historically been low risk, steady return with a long time horizon, and expectations of a 5% return on capital. In our financialised form of capitalism, privatisation and outsourcing bring in stock market quoted corporates, private equity houses and fund investors with market-driven requirements for a return of more than 10%, and business models developed in high risk, high return, short time horizon activities. Returns can be levered up in the short term by financial engineering devices, investment rationing, tax avoidance, asset stripping and loading enterprises with debt. Meanwhile power is used to boost revenue by confusion pricing, and to reduce costs by hitting on stakeholders who account for a major part of costs (like labour in adult care or suppliers in supermarkets).

Chapter 4 turns to moral and political argument about the rights and duties of citizens. The third and fourth chapters are connected because, when corporations are juridical persons, they are citizens just as much as natural persons. Corporations as citizens have duties, but these are commonly abrogated by their predatory behaviour in the foundational economy. Our argument, then, is that the duties of corporate citizens should be made explicit through a process of political bargaining which brings the operations of privately owned companies into the public domain under a reformed constitution. And reforming the constitution is not a marginal matter: it involves rethinking in a fundamental way the relations between private enterprise and the state. Under a system of social licence, modelled on the agreements between mining companies and indigenous communities, all companies which draw revenue from the foundational economy would have to specify what they put back as social benefit into the relevant communities.

Chapter 4 also tackles the question of how to understand 'social citizenship' or the entitlements of natural persons. The experience since the 1980s refutes T.H. Marshall's progressive assumption that citizen entitlement to foundational services will grow from one period to the next. Equally, citizen entitlements within Europe vary by country or region and many in the adjacent Middle East or North Africa are excluded from the benefits we take for granted. It is therefore important to show that there is a core to citizenship which can be detached from territory. Put another way, the foundational project (of expanding human capabilities and establishing the conditions of flourishing) needs to take account of others, including unborn generations. But citizenship can then only become material within a new political practice – the theme of Chapter 5.

The starting point of Chapter 5 is that foundational thinking overlaps with recent discussion of universal basic provision of income, infrastructure and services, though these are still tied up with top-down concepts of policymaking and are not always clear about who should get what and why. In a first major clarification, Chapter 5 lays out four key shifts which would together change the paradigm of policymaking: obtain participation by asking citizens about their foundational priorities; extend social influence over business by licensing corporate business and encouraging small and medium-sized private and social enterprises; refinance the state by reinventing taxation to secure foundational revenue and capital investment; and, finally, create hybrid political alliances for change to drive public policy on the basis that government is not always benign or capable.

These conditions indicate a clear direction of travel and the good news is that radical change does not wait upon perfect alignment of political preconditions to deliver the four shifts. The chapter ends with a proposal for local and regional experiments which would make the foundational visible, debatable and actionable, and which can gain momentum and scale if supported at national and supranational level. These would be disruptive, mobilising experiments of the kind envisaged by Roberto Unger as radical social innovation, not 'what works' experiments, which allow established power to negotiate the world more intelligently. From such radical experiments can come learning and political mobilisation that begins to shift constraints.

Finally, it should be noted that this book about social consumption is itself a collective production. As noted in the Acknowledgements, the book was directly authored by a gang of five: the text was drafted and redrafted by Mick Moran and Karel Williams, who were closely advised and prompted on structural decisions, shaping of the argument and exhibits for each chapter by Julie Froud, Sukhdev Johal and Angelo Salento. Other members of the foundational collective contributed notes and drafts for chapters within book plans which were hammered out by the whole group in three seminar meetings in Turin, London and Lecce. The stock of ideas is collective and the creativity and scope of the book's argument owes everything to the group.

The collective includes academics of many different nationalities and regional identities, who all wanted to write a short book that would be of broad relevance to European citizens. Limits of space and available case material meant that we could not do justice to the diversity of Europe, let alone explore differences in other countries beyond. We also did not always succeed in finding the language to discuss complex issues in an accessible way. But we hope our audience will fill in some of the gaps and develop our argument so that this book can mark a new beginning in the story of the foundational economy.

The members of the Foundational Economy collective are: Davide Arcidiacono, Filippo Barbera, Andrew Bowman, John Buchanan, Sandro Busso, Joselle Dagnes, Joe Earle, Ewald Engelen, Peter Folkman, Julie Froud, Colin Haslam, Sukhdev Johal, Ian Rees Jones, Dario Minervini, Mick Moran, Fabio Mostaccio, Gabriella Pauli, Leonhard Plank, Angelo Salento, Ferdinando Spina, Nick Tsitsianis, Karel Williams.

2 (Re)discovering the foundational

The morning routine

You get the children to school and then get yourself to work on a weekday morning in any European city. After the alarm sounds, on with the bedside light before taking the shower that wakes you up; breakfast is bread and some milk from the supermarket, with the milk warmed on the stove, because that's the way both children like it. Your mother's carer rings to say she cannot make the home visit today. You go online to check your bank balance because it's the third week of the month, and then you order an overdue service for the boiler. The kids are squabbling again as you walk them briskly to the neighbourhood primary school just across the park. Then you catch the bus for the twenty-minute commute to the city centre where you have a job as a medical technician in the big teaching hospital.

We could vary the domestic circumstances by adding a partner, and the cultural details of the routine would vary according to time and place. The British parent typically starts the day with a cup of tea after boiling an electric kettle; the Italian parent traditionally makes a cup of coffee in a stove-top moka pot. Convenience and time pressures since the 1950s are reflected in Britain with the victory of the tea bag over loose leaf and tea pot, or in Italy since the 1980s with the rise of the coffee capsule. If we shift out of region to the US or Japan, practice varies, as there are different ways of achieving the same ends. For example, in America, half the children get to school on dedicated yellow buses; in provincial Japan, they can be marched to school in a crocodile with older children acting as marshals.

But that is the here and now. Everyday life was not like this for most of human history and it is not like this for many people in low-income countries today. Through most of history, cities were so unhealthy that they relied on inward migration to maintain population. That is what it was like before about 1880 in large West European cities plagued by high infant mortality and infectious diseases (Lenger 2012, pp. 38–40). Disease killed rich and poor alike because cities did not have urban systems which piped clean water and sanitation to every household and distributed gas and electricity for convenience. These absences still shape a parent's daily routine in a South African township or a Mumbai slum. For most of human history, and in many poor communities now, the waking parent fumbles to light a candle or an oil lamp, and a first task is to fetch or draw water. If unclean water makes you ill, there is no entitlement to free healthcare. Schooling has to be paid for – a cost beyond the purse of the poor.

Household exclusion from utility supply and/or illegal access to these supplies is still commonplace in lower-income countries. In South Africa, for instance, less than half of households have water piped to the dwelling;[1] one quarter of households report interruption of supply;[2] and 27% lack sanitation that meets the World Health Organization (WHO) basic level.[3] Electricity theft is widespread in South Africa: Eskom, the South African electricity utility estimates that the country loses at least 20 billion rand a year through theft.[4] And across much of Latin America the challenge is to provide supply of water and electricity at affordable prices. Many favelas rely on illegal standpipes and unmetered household electricity connection: the official estimate is that 13% of all electricity generated in Brazil is 'stolen' and it is as high as 30% in Amazonas state.[5]

The organisation of effective, universal providential services like health and education is as much of a challenge for many poor and middle-income countries. South Africa spends more than 5% of GDP on education (which is more than the EU average) but 27% of children cannot read after attending school for six years.[6] The problems here are as much about organisation and income distribution as about per capita average income level. At least one low-income, socialist country has universal medical services which produce excellent outcomes: Cuba has lower infant mortality than the US and Cuban life expectancy of seventy-nine is thirty years higher than in neighbouring Haiti.[7] But in most poor and middle-income countries, health services are exiguous for those who cannot pay privately.

By way of contrast, between 7am and 9am every workday morning in Europe most citizens use goods and services that draw on more than six economic and social systems which are the everyday infrastructure of civilised life. In the opening example, our working parent actually uses and relies on at least 11 different services before starting work as a medical technician in the hospital. In order of use in our example they are: electricity supply; piped water; waste water and sewerage; retail food supply; domestic piped gas; telecommunications (copper wire and mobile); adult care; retail banking; consumer durable maintenance; education; and public transport.

These services and systems are not only mundane. They are usually taken for granted until they fail, for instance when unsafe food or power cuts are front page crises. Then, civil servants and politicians must fix things because citizens in high-income countries expect to eat safe food and to keep the lights on. Continuity of supply is taken for granted, so that occasional interruptions are met with puzzlement, as in South Australia recently where vox pop responses included: 'it's 2017 – surely we're past power outages and have back-ups' and 'it's definitely weird for a first world country not to have reliable power sources all the time' (ABC News 2017). Citizens know they are living in a failed state like Libya when they have to put up with endless power cuts (Sherib and Sorrer 2017).

These mundane but essential services are not entirely taken for granted in rich capitalist democracies. Problems about quality, access and pricing of these systems and services clatter around in political debate; as indeed has the question of their public or private sector ownership and operation. Since the rise of free market ideologies like Thatcherism we have had, in many countries, privatisation of the utilities which were previously state owned. More recently we have had outsourcing of tax-funded services like adult care which were previously directly provided by the state. These developments are resisted by unionised labour and create disquiet amongst citizens about the size of their utility bills and the quality of social services provided.

However, these services are treated very partially in mainstream economic thinking and policy debate. Here 'infrastructure' is viewed narrowly as a lever for economic regeneration and competitiveness. Training or educating the workforce and adding (physical) transport infrastructure are the two standard prescriptions for improving job creation and economic growth of laggard regions. We could take illustrative quotes from EU, national or regional economic plans. For example, here is an economic strategy document from the Greater Manchester city region from the first half of the 2010s, when it aligned with the UK Treasury by buying into this orthodoxy:

> The key to sharing prosperity is in ensuring that more of our people are able to access the labour market, remain in work and develop the skills to progress within that labour market, improving both productivity and self-sufficiency and reducing demand for public services ... Greater Manchester has consistently placed connectivity and transport investment at the heart of our economic strategy ... This investment strengthens and

widens GM's labour market, which is crucial to our future
success and enables GM businesses to reduce costs by moving
people and goods more quickly, easily and reliably. (GMCA
2013, pp. 23, 34)

That gives us an impoverished view of the scope and importance
of a kind of invisible economy whose goods and services lie
at the foundation of everyday civilised life.

The singular economy: GDP and knowledge-intensive business services

The roots of this invisibility lie in the way academic economic
language, and the policymakers who borrow from it, think
and talk about 'the economy'. They construct a field of the
visible – and as a result make important things invisible.
Although there are many kinds of economics (mainstream
and heterodox) in our time, they generally share a view of
the world in which the services and systems that concern us
in this book do not exist as a discrete object of thought and
action.

As with other discourses, economics reveals as it conceals
through rhetorical devices. In this case the two classical devices
are metaphor and metonymy. Through metaphor, the concept
of GDP and growth has, for over fifty years, created an image
of a singular economy: the metric brackets heterogeneous
parts of economic life as alike, on the basis that they all create
market income which can be added up by economists. At the
same time, through metonymy, the part is taken for the whole.
Economists and policymakers have for the past thirty years
increasingly focused on the competitive and high-tech part of
the economy, and mundane activities have vanished from view.

The problems of GDP thinking are well known. National
income accounting was developed during the Second World
War in the US and UK as part of mobilisation for total war

so that US policymakers could judge the balance between
military and civilian output and the UK policymakers could
curb inflation at full employment output levels. Early GDP
developers like Kuznets (1934) and recent critics like Fioramonti
(2013; 2017) and Coyle (2014) agree that GDP is a poor
guide to welfare. The process of adding up market incomes
and government output at cost is beset with technical problems,
like how to count defence expenditure or value the output of
the financial sector; while feminists and green critics have
raised larger issues about unpaid work and environmental
externalities.[8]

There is, in any case, a large practical discrepancy between
the kinds of welfare that concern us in this book and GDP.
That point has been dramatised since 1990 by the UN Human
Development Index which, in its earliest simplest form, ranked
countries by combining three indicators of GDP: using the
Gross National Income (GNI) measure, life expectancy and
years of schooling. While there is an overall positive correlation
between GDP and the other variables, the relation is very
weak in middle-income countries. These countries have hugely
variable political capacity to organise public health systems
which deliver increased life expectancy or to mobilise fiscal
resources which fund many years of schooling (Deb 2015).

And yet the GDP measure survives as a way in which policymakers talk amongst themselves and politicians address an
uncomprehending public. 'The fastest rate of GDP growth in
the G7 or G20' is a matter of bragging rights for the finance
minister in your country; and every European finance minister
can hope to get lucky in claiming this achievement when
economic cycles in different national economies are not
synchronised. Few in the political classes notice that this talk
of GDP and growth rates is at best mood music in news
bulletins and political campaigns, because many ordinary
citizens have a very blurred understanding of what the categories mean. In a recent British survey, only 39% of respondents
could define GDP and 25% simply ticked 'don't know' (Earle,

Moran and Ward-Perkins 2017, p. 19). The position is likely to be much the same in other countries.

The debate about replacing the GDP metric has not been brought to a conclusion because it opens onto a post Human Development Index discussion about balanced scorecards and welfare dashboards with multiple indicators, as proposed by Stiglitz, Sen and Fitou's report for the European Commission (Stiglitz, Sen and Fitoussi 2009). These are technically interesting but would be intellectually challenging for the ordinary citizen when asked to engage with a news story about improvements in, say, three of five key welfare indicators. And at the same time, it is very easy for such discussions to get bogged down in the details of average performance against target and lose sight of Richard Titmuss' great insight that welfare means 'minimum standards for all citizens' – an argument more recently echoed in the concept of 'sufficiency' that underpins the Bhutan experiment in replacing GDP. Minimum standards are important because despite a formal commitment to the universal service principle, in practice there can be 'poor public services for poor people';[9] debates about access should focus on quality for all, not simply on the safety net of a residual service.

Against this background of discussion about broadening measures, there has recently been a narrowing of the policy field of vision onto the component of GDP generated by one part of the market economy, knowledge-intensive business services (KIBS) and high-tech manufacturing. This is a very recent and powerful rethinking of the economy, which represents a kind of defensive response by the European policy community to deteriorating economic performance and growing insecurity. For example, the term 'knowledge-intensive business services' to denote services employing well-qualified professionals and scientists was first used in a report by Miles *et al.* (1995) to the EU. The preoccupation with promoting innovation through state support of research and development is more recent and in the UK owes much to Mazzucato (2015) and growing receptiveness to arguments about market failure in supporting early stage innovation. A typical result is the British Government's proposed UK industrial policy of 2017, which promises that 'new "sector deals" and investment in research and development will support the industries of the future where Britain has the potential to lead the world – from electric vehicles to biotech and quantum technologies' (UK Government 2017).

This preoccupation with KIBS and advanced manufacturing is understandable. These are intrinsically desirable, glamorous, next-generation industries: high-tech, high value added and high-paid, employing an educated workforce. More immediately, in a world of slowing growth and European uncompetitiveness, these industries are seen as carriers of innovation, high productivity and renewal through competitivity. Thus EU civil servants and national or regional politicians, and their economic advisors, draw the inference that it is crucial to support these 'next-generation' sectors for the economic benefits they bring. But this is optimistic because these sectors are very small in terms of direct employment. This can be demonstrated in an intelligible way by considering the volume of EU employment in KIBS and high-tech manufacturing and making the comparison with health and social care. Across the 28 EU countries, high-tech manufacturing and knowledge-intensive high-tech services currently employ no more than 4% of the workforce, and the range of national variation is between 2.2% in Lithuania and 7.4% in Ireland.[10]

This issue about the limited employment base remains if we broaden the definition and argue that medium-tech manufacturing is a next-generation activity. If we remade every EU country in the image of Germany and added together KIBS, high-tech manufacturing and medium-tech manufacturing, which includes engineering, then all three sectors would employ no more than 10%. The number employed in 'knowledge intensive activities' is much larger and growing but that is a statistical confusion. These activities are defined by their employment of graduates, and the supply of graduates is dramatically increasing simply because 40% of the age cohort in many European countries now attend university. The result is that many traditionally non-graduate roles are being filled by workers with a first degree: for example, in the UK in 2017, 49% of recent graduates and 37% of those who graduated more than five years earlier were working in 'non-graduate' roles (ONS 2017).

Employment in next-generation industries would have to grow at a heroic rate for a sustained period before they could deliver on the hopes and dreams of national policymakers. Even with sustained growth, it is unlikely that they could then deliver international competitive success for many or all EU countries. If many national governments are targeting the same sectors, we cannot all succeed nationally in capturing value as exporters of KIBS. And again, even with sustained expansion, these services will certainly not create jobs for the school leavers who do not go to university, or create jobs for many local residents in the districts where they expand. Meanwhile, the aura around KIBS feeds a Europe-wide competition to capture mobile KIBS activity through incentives and concessions. This produces all kinds of distortions, as with 'race to the bottom' tax competition led by countries like Ireland, so that these activities are then everywhere lightly taxed and make a limited contribution to the funding of the public services that benefit all citizens.

In sum, the preoccupation with KIBS and high-tech means that policymakers picture the economy like an iceberg: the small glamorous high-tech part is visible to economic policymakers, while a large, important part is below the surface and invisible. The simplest way of demonstrating this point and opening up the related intellectual and political issues is to count the numbers employed in education and health care as 'eds and meds' and imagine how to think of universities and hospitals as engines of city region development (Bartik and Erickcek 2008).

If we leave education out of the picture, and just consider health and social care, the economic size and social welfare linkages from these sectors are obvious. Across the 28 EU countries, 'health and social work' together employ 10.9% of the workforce; the range is from 6.5% in Hungary to 14.6% in France. And there are two key social linkages from these sectors. First, these sectors employ diverse skills: hospitals need multiple specialists including paramedics, nurses, doctors, technicians, pharmacists, radiographers and so on; while adult care offers responsible and meaningful jobs, including to those who have few qualifications. These care workers will often also be ill-trained and underpaid because there are many disconnects in our society between social usefulness, educational certification and pay. Second, health and social care are important because they provide essential services which are meshed with the rights of being a European citizen; if health service delivery fails we immediately have a huge crisis of welfare which is much graver and more difficult to manage than any difficulties following failure of, say, civil legal services.

But health and social care are not seen by the European political classes and policymakers as core productive activities within the economy. Instead (publicly funded) health and education are the domain of social policies which determine availability and quality of service, so that only their funding through taxes will concern the economics or finance ministry.

This compartmentalisation of activity is part of the new physiocracy. The original physiocrats were the eighteenth-century French economists who believed that wealth was derived from land and that only agricultural production created a surplus so that industry and trade was unproductive and surplus consuming. The new physiocrats are the twenty-first-century European politicians who suppose that private sector, market-based activities are wealth-creating, while health, social care and other public services are surplus consuming. The standard official argument is that growth of GDP is the answer and that we can only fund activities like health and social care indirectly (and safeguard everything else) by growing market income through competitive success with tradeables in international markets. Here, for example, is a centre-right British minister of health (Jeremy Hunt) explaining how tax cuts can actually be good for the National Health Service (NHS), which he sees as outside 'the economy':

> Corporation taxes are being cut so that we can boost jobs and strengthen the economy so that we can fund the NHS. The reason we've been able to protect and increase funding in the NHS in the last six years ... is precisely because we've created two million jobs and we've given this country the fastest growing economy in the G7.[11]

It is both plausibly true and fundamentally misleading that health, social care and other European public services are surplus consuming not wealth-producing. Plausibly true because they are tax-funded; fundamentally misleading because the line between tax revenue producing and consuming can be changed by legislative fiat as privatisation and nationalisation move activities between state and private sector. We live in a world where the private sector taxes of mobile phone companies and other corporate enterprises pay for doctors' salaries; but this world would be turned upside down if the state nationalised mobile companies and privatised healthcare because taxes on hospitals would then pay for the salaries in the mobile company's call centre (Harford 2011). If that counterfactual is too challenging, consider whether the pending privatisation of Italian railways will at a stroke increase national wealth or welfare. It would be more sensible to think of 'the economy' not as a system of wealth creation led by the private sector but a system of revenue circulation which should diffuse welfare.

Recognising multiplicity: the idea of the foundational economy

Knowing all this, our problem was how to reframe the economy and bring into focus those large parts which are invisible or only semi-visible in official economic policy. As our background was in empirically resourceful and conceptually minimalist research, we did not turn to theorised political economy but to the economic and social history of Fernand Braudel. In the 1970s, Braudel had faced a similar problem about how to challenge historians who wanted to rewrite the economic history of the early modern period as the history of GDP growth and the market dynamic which delivered Western industrialism and imperialism.

In the first volume of *Civilization and Capitalism*, Braudel (1981) described the 'structures of everyday life', arguing that from the fifteenth to the eighteenth century there were two further economic zones, one above and one below the market. Most of the world's population lived in a quite different, mundane and slow-moving *infra economy* of 'material life'. This was organised around immediate production and consumption rather than exchange. At the same time, above the market was a *supra economy* of a few merchants and financiers engaged in long distance trade and speculation (1981, p. 23). Braudel's three-level scheme is specific to the early modern period, but his strategy of recognising a layer cake multiplicity and diversity in the economy resonates today.

In 2013, we proposed the idea of a 'foundational economy' producing welfare-critical goods and services like housing, education, childcare, healthcare and utility supply (Bentham *et al.* 2013). The sphere of the foundational was then demarcated by three criteria: these goods and services were necessary to everyday life; were consumed daily by all citizens regardless of income; and were distributed according to population through branches and networks. They were partly non-market, generally sheltered and one way or another politically franchised.

Instead of the glamour economy of KIBS and high-tech tradeables, we were then concerned with a mundane economy which was neglected and not the object of policy except insofar as retreating states privatised and outsourced activities for short-term gains. The original concept was good enough to shift the field of the visible. Since then, we have added refinement to recognise the heterogeneity of what is inside this foundational economy by discriminating between material and providential activities, rather than jumbling them together. This gives us a number of domains of the foundational economy, which are practically important in different ways.

The first, the *material foundational economy* is labelled thus for an obvious reason: it consists classically of the pipes and cables, networks and branches which continuously connect households to daily essentials – like water, electricity, retail banking and food – where interruption of supply results in immediate crisis. There is also another critical feature of this domain: it generates a revenue stream from households and, as a result, in recent decades private provision or privatisation of state provision has proved an attractive policy option.

Up to around the last quarter of the nineteenth century across almost all of what would now be considered the advanced capitalist democracies, virtually everyone worked in economies that exacted a huge toll in physical effort; lived in domestic circumstances where everyday tasks like cooking and washing involved endless drudgery; and on average died soon after their fortieth birthday (Deaton 2014, p. 83). The material foundational economy after 1880 transformed the physical conditions and the productivity of paid labour, and the daily conditions of domestic life, as Gordon has so vividly documented in his account of the rise of the 'networked household' (Gordon 2016). When combined with revolutionary changes in understandings of public health and clinical medicine, it also transformed the health and longevity of whole populations.

Some of the conditions of that transformation – like the reservoirs that serve our great cities – were visible from space, but most were an invisible underground network of pipes and cables. With digital technologies, part of this is now dematerialising as mobile signals replace copper or fibre wires within and to each household. These changes were paralleled by another set of changes in material conditions, as action at a distance created longer and more complex food supply chains, initially through railways and steam ships. For the first time in history they have removed the populations of the high-income countries from the local and regional pressure of a bad harvest and high prices and created a huge corporate food supply sector: there are 29 supermarkets in the global top 100 chains by turnover, with Walmart, Carrefour and Tesco all in the list of the top five largest global retail chains.[12]

A second domain, the *providential foundational economy*, is labelled thus because it turned the state into a source of providential good fortune through (mainly) public-sector welfare activity providing universal services – like health and education – and income transfer available to all citizens. Its provision is now increasingly outsourced in some countries, but still heavily dependent on state funding or financing because it is either typically means-tested or free-at-point-of-use.

The providential foundational economy was largely the creation of state intervention in the century after 1870 across a wide range of jurisdictions. Beginning with the innovations in social policy in Bismarck's Germany, states created legal entitlements to incomes and services: unemployment insurance, free school education, pensions in old age, free healthcare. In the three decades after the end of the Second World War most of the states of Western Europe expanded and completed this project, one that amounted to the creation of a parallel *providential* set of goods and services to stand alongside the material foundational economy. We usually understand this, more social, infrastructure as a welfare state.

The combination of the two categories of goods and services – delivered by the material and the providential infrastructures – have a double significance because they both create a foundational economy and are central to the entitlements of citizenship in the modern state. Providential services have historically been enmeshed with the idea of social citizenship; but, in practice, access to utility services like domestic energy and clean water also amount to basic citizenship entitlements. Consider the imaginary family whose daily routine began this chapter. The 11 foundational services we identified, from clean water to free school education, are entitlements regardless of income, job or any mark of status. We know that, in practice, the quality of service often varies, but our society is organised on the assumption that basic entitlements can be claimed by all. Thus the foundational economy gains a moral significance, for providential and material together establish our everyday notions of what constitute the basic human needs that must to be met to ensure that lives can be lived to their full potential.

Why is it important to discriminate the foundational economy and its constituent parts? Here are three good reasons.

- Foundational provision is welfare-critical for users because limited material and providential access stunts lives and limits possibilities. This is something we have lost sight of through our preoccupation with income measures of poverty. For many citizens, the relevant welfare considerations will be the cost and availability of housing, pricing of fuel and public transport and access to specialist services like mental health. In many cases, it would be sensible to start any kind of politics from an inventory of foundational provision and an inquiry into citizen needs and wants.
- Foundational goods and services are generally matters of social provision where branch and network structure (plus subsidy and cost recovery considerations) typically determine possibilities of individual household consumption. The individual citizen can buy a smartphone, but its usefulness

depends on 4G network coverage in a region. Network or branch provision is typically decided by supermarkets or health services according to some calculation of demand according to population and users, related to norms on minimal provision and cross-subsidy, which can vary considerably.

• The production of foundational goods and services employs large numbers of workers in activities which are typically sheltered from international competition so that, for example, working conditions can be determined locally. This is true in all regions of all high-income countries, as we demonstrate in the exhibits that follow with a national comparison between Germany, the UK and Italy and a city region comparison between London and Liverpool as a successful global city and deindustrialised port.

Data on employment in foundational activities cannot give a precise measure. The general problem is that the foundational economy can only be measured through official statistics, whose categories were devised for other purposes and only partly correspond with the distinctions we want to make. In the case of employment, for example, the assignments are partly to activities, like pharmacy where the demand is partly social and foundational for prescription medicines and partly individual and lifestyle for cosmetics. So, employees in a particular activity have to be allocated to the foundational according to judgement. Appendix 2.1 gives a reasoned account of some of our major classification decisions. More information on the major employment categories, using NACE and SIC classifications,[13] are explained in the relevant section of the foundationaleconomy.com web site.[14]

When these qualifications have been entered, the employment statistics are revealing of the weight and significance of the foundational. In all high-income countries, the material and providential together account for more than one third and less than one half of employment. Exhibit 2.1 presents national comparisons of the share of material and providential

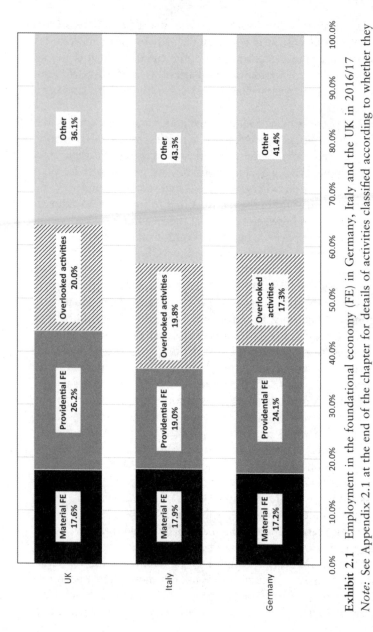

Exhibit 2.1 Employment in the foundational economy (FE) in Germany, Italy and the UK in 2016/17

Note: See Appendix 2.1 at the end of the chapter for details of activities classified according to whether they are material, providential or overlooked.

Sources: Bundesagentur für Arbeit, ISTAT and ONS.

employment which together account for 41.3% of German employment, 43.8% of UK employment and 36.9% of Italian employment. In all three countries, material activities account for just over 17% of total employment and the variation is accounted for by the share of providential activities which at 19% in Italy is substantially lower than the 26.2% share in the UK. (The exhibits below also present data on the 'overlooked economy', a category which will be explained shortly.)

Within each country there is a range of internal variation. Cities and regions which are successful in international trade and the national division of functions typically have substantially lower shares of material plus providential employment than in deindustrialised or agricultural regions where population related foundational employment is the crucial remaining regional support. In the UK, the most successful region, London, has the lowest percentage with a material plus providential share of 35%; all other regions are above 40%, and deindustrialised peripheral regions like the North East of England have the highest percentage share, with material plus providential accounting for around 50%. These differences are clearly caused by the presence of multiple other sources of employment in London and the loss of manufacturing and heavy industrial jobs from areas like the North East, which are then more dependent on the foundational jobs that remain. This point demonstrated in Exhibit 2.2, which compares London with the city region of Liverpool, where material and providential account for almost exactly 50% of employment.

The split between providential and material employment and the activity sources of foundational employment are again striking. If we take the UK case, nationally there are three workers employed in the providential to every two in the material, and that ratio is reasonably constant with London as something of an outlier. More interesting are the activity sources of foundational employment. Half of material employment is accounted for by activities directly serving the networked

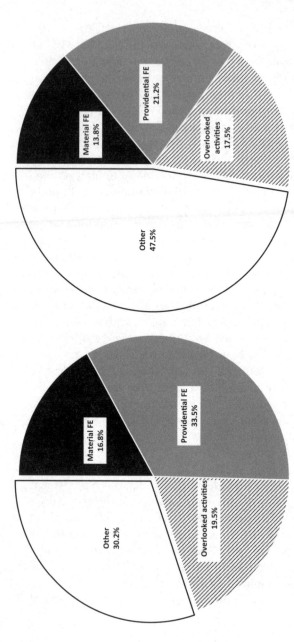

Exhibit 2.2a Employment in Liverpool city region in 2016

Exhibit 2.2b Employment in London in 2016

Note: see Appendix 2.1 at the end of the chapter for details of activities classified according to whether they are material, providential or overlooked.

Source: ONS.

household; sale of food and drink accounts for 25% of material employment while pipe and cable utilities and transport account for another 25%. Providential employment is dominated by education, medicine and social care: compulsory and tertiary education together account for nearly 30% of the providential workforce, primary and secondary healthcare for just over 30%, and social care for another 20%.

It is important to underline the point that the boundaries of the foundational economy are imprecise because they are economically blurred and politically contested. This point can be demonstrated by considering the question of housing. In common-sense terms, housing appears to be foundational because every household needs a roof over its head at an affordable price (whether rented or owned). But the economic visibility of that need depends on the way that the foundational economy is measured; and the political recognition of that housing need depends on political struggle. These measurements and political issues are discussed below.

In the examples above, the foundational was measured in employment terms, where housing does not figure prominently because most of us live in an already constructed house which requires only occasional maintenance labour. However, the foundational economy can also be measured by considering the objects of household expenditure, as disclosed in national household surveys. Exhibit 2.3 presents data on average weekly household expenditure in the EU 28 in 2016. Again, the survey categories do not exactly suit the purpose of foundational analysis. But it is instructive to compare all actual housing costs (rent and/or mortgage payments) with total household spend on what we have classified as essential items plus mobility. On this rough basis, actual housing costs of €109.50 per week account for 42% of essential expenditure and 33% of expenditure essentials plus mobility. It is equally interesting to note that the items we have classified under the essentials and mobility subheadings account for no less than 47% of all weekly expenditure.

Households everywhere must spend money on renting or buying housing, but the recognition of housing as a foundational need depends on political struggle which does not have an inevitable outcome. In some high-income countries housing has never been recognised as a social necessity; in others there has been a move towards treating housing as a household asset and source of individual wealth. At one extreme, 42% of dwellings in Vienna are social housing (25% owned by the city of Vienna and 17% by non-profit organisations); the corresponding figure in Australia is 5% (4% in public housing and 1% in community housing) (Martin, Pawson and van den Nouwelant 2016). Within a single state there can be large-scale sale and conversion of social housing into private asset, as in the UK where 'right-to-buy' since 1980 has removed 1.8 million houses from the social stock, without replacement from new construction.[15] These examples show that while the foundational economy can appear almost as an unacknowledged part of the natural order of things, in some cases, the extent of provision (volume, quality and means of access) is the result of protracted political struggles.

The domains of the foundational economy that most concern us in this book are the material and providential. But however far the boundaries of the foundational are pushed, there will be an outer domain, an *overlooked economy* of lifestyle and comfort support systems, which are occasionally purchased out of discretionary income but nevertheless arise from established cultural expectations. In Europe, we all expect to be able to visit a hairdresser or to buy a sofa for the living room. We call this the overlooked economy because policymakers and the media focus attention elsewhere on more glamorous activities. In Wales, some 3,000 workers are engaged in sofa production for all the major retail chains, while a similar number work in steel making at the Port Talbot plant of Tata-Thyssen Krupp. But sofa workers are completely invisible, whereas every twist and turn in the steel plant's fortunes

Exhibit 2.3   Average weekly household expenditure in the EU 28 countries in 2015

	EU 28 household expenditure per week
Food and non-alcoholic drinks	€86.98
Actual housing rents and mortgage costs and related costs	€109.50
Water supply and miscellaneous services	€17.77
Electricity, gas and other fuels	€28.38
Communication	€18.13
Total spend on essential items	**€260.77**
Transport services (rail, bus etc. excluding air travel)	€27.96
Operation of personal transport	€44.81
Total spend on mobility	**€72.77**
Total spend on essentials and mobility	**€333.54**
Total Expenditure	**€711.27**
Essential item expenditure and mobility expenditure as a % of total expenditure	46.9%
Number of households (m)	219.9

Source: Eurostat http://ec.europa.eu/eurostat/statistics-explained/index.php/Household_consumption_by_purpose.

attract national attention, with ministers in London actively engaged with the corporate owners.

This oversight is unjustified. We all need clothing, furniture like beds and sofas, central heating and/or cooling, house maintenance, body maintenance including hairdressing, pet food and vet services, leisure and tourism and hospitality – and at the end of it all we may not want but will need a funeral. Haircuts and sofas are not a matter of network connections and do not fit into the material or providential categories, but they do matter. Imagine that the invented family with which we began this chapter could never visit a hairdresser, could not afford a sofa for the living room, never had a holiday from work, and at the end of it all could not afford a dignified funeral. Impoverished people like these exist in all advanced capitalist democracies, but their condition violates the cultural norms of those societies.

One implication of this analysis of foundational domains and an overlooked outer domain, is that, over time, boundaries are not fixed, because goods and services move into and between categories. Within the lived experience of one or two generations, luxuries become cultural necessities: in the past fifty years, central heating in Northern Europe or air conditioning in Australia have become domestic necessities. More subtly, luxuries can become citizen entitlements, as in the case of adult care. One hundred years ago, when the middle classes were defined by their employment of domestic servants, they could buy-in care in many forms from domestic companion to skivvy; now citizens of many European cities take it for granted that they can telephone social services and request help, which will also be free for low income groups.

The historically contingent nature of these final examples makes an important point about the foundational economy. When we make the foundational economy visible, we are not discovering a thing but assembling a construct that serves a socio-political purpose. The foundational economy changes what is visible when we talk about economic life. It puts into high visibility the numerous goods and services that underpin our lives but that we barely think about from day to day. It has the added virtue of acting as a corrective to the mania for grand projects, high-technology industries and educational certification that obsess policymakers, and it restores the importance of unappreciated and unacknowledged tacit skills of many citizens, like those who care for others.

At various points we have previously described the foundational economy as mundane. But a shallow, showy world does not respond positively to the use of descriptors like mundane or modest; such descriptors can also create the misleading impression that the foundational economy is part of a low-technology world. Some of the foundational economy is itself high-tech: as with electricity generation and distribution, which has been at the leading edge of innovation for more than 100 years. And much that is mundane incorporates technology – as with food processing, which is probably the largest purchaser of machinery in most advanced economies, or food retailing, where the supermarket chains pioneered electronic point of sales systems and use of big data, as well as developing highly sophisticated logistics in their supply chains.

But, more important, we would not want to try to over-sell the foundational economy on the basis of its association with high-tech, because the idea of the foundational represents a fundamental change of perspective on technology. Most discussion of technology proceeds from the view point of the innovator who builds an industry; thus, European national policymakers are obsessed with trying to turn innovation into competitive international industries, while Silicon Valley platform builders are concerned with monetising innovation. Against this, foundational thinking adopts the technology user perspective advocated by Edgerton (2008). The foundational opportunity is to integrate new technology into social activities like adult care by users who bricolage old and new.

The foundational economy is a social construct and, like any social construct is always the subject of political contestation. This is especially true of the providential domain because the extent of state recognition of social need is very variable. More broadly, the provision of foundational goods and services (and the underlying state funding) is a highly valuable prize over which powerful interests will continuously struggle. That is part of the starting point of this book. In the last generation the way the material and the providential are organised has been transformed. The political coalitions that established the providential as a set of citizenship entitlements have been in retreat in the face of incursions by market ideologues who opened the way for corporate interests seeking double digit returns on capital. The organisational structures of whole areas of the material – like public utilities – have been transformed by corporate delivery and fund ownership. In short, the foundational economy has a socio-political history which we consider in the next section.

A short history of the foundational economy

The foundational, as described in the previous section, is the broad social infrastructure of safe and civilised life. Our ideas of infrastructure have been narrowed by mainstream economics where infrastructure is what makes the labour market or the economy work: hence the preoccupation with travel-to-work transport and with systems like fast broadband for business users. In foundational thinking, the concern is with the broader, multiple uses of such systems: for example, transport systems bring mobility which is used for social purposes as much as for commuting. And we are concerned with a much broader range of systems, including, for example, care homes and income support, which are infrastructure that makes everyday life work just as much as does a tram system. These infra-structural systems represent both socio-technic innovation – pipes, cables and national insurance contribution systems – and political achievement, which depended on alliances of political forces that could in the 1880s or the 1940s mobilise the power to overcome opposing interests and resistance to expenditure on basic services.

Much of the socio-technic was nearly once-and-for-all innovation and investment which could (with patching) last many generations. The Vrnwy dam, which pioneered water over-spilling a stone retainer wall, was completed in 1888 and (with new pipe work) this dam still supplies Liverpool with water. The English national grid of high voltage transmission, which was completed in 1933, replaced an inefficient and fragmented system of local generation. That grid (with maintenance and extension) will last until low-cost distributed power generation-cum-storage systems are developed in the next generation. But the political alignments were always conjunctural and (as we now know) reversible because the foundational economy does not have an inbuilt ratchet mechanism which consolidates progress: the history of the foundational economy is not a Whig history of citizens gaining ever more rights and recognition of needs.

Thus, in cartoon form, the history of the foundational economy has three moments. The first heroic municipal phase centred on the physical engineering of gas and water in Europe in the last half of the nineteenth century – along with public transport and housing in some cities – which set in train a material transformation of life chances, life quality and everyday life experience.[16] The second national triumph of *Les Trente Glorieuses* – the thirty glorious years in Europe after the Second World War – then added providential income support, free social and healthcare, free education and a host of other services for whole populations. But that achievement contained the seeds of its undermining after 1980 in a new conjuncture when an impoverished state could be preyed upon by financial engineers. What the central state gave, it could also take away; and the material and providential were, in an increasingly financialised capitalism, an attractive source of saleable assets and predictable cash flows.

Town gas and water were at the forefront of a new urban order in the last quarter of the nineteenth century. Municipal gas supply was everywhere because it could be produced relatively easily from coal in a scalable way using coke ovens, and distributed locally through small bore piping to deliver new amenities like the gas-lit city streets of the 1880s. Water and sanitation in large cities represented a civil engineering challenge because water supply required the construction of large reservoirs; and the management of waste water required large-scale underground construction of sewers. The two imperatives meant that the monumental foundational projects of this period were the reservoirs and the sewerage systems. These are epitomised by Eugene Belgrand's work on the Paris sewer system after 1852 or Joseph Bazalgette's intercepting sewer system constructed after 1859 to dispose of London's waste into the Thames estuary.

Belgrand was Director of Water and Sewers of Paris under Baron Haussmann and Bazalgette was Chief Engineer of the Metropolitan Board of Works. Their titles alert us to the second feature of this first phase of the foundational economy: it was led by municipalities. The smaller municipalities moved slowly because, as late as 1895, 42% of Prussian urban communities with over 2,000 inhabitants lacked mains water (Evans 1987, p. 146). But the initiative was municipal so that in the German Empire of 1909, 93% of the waterworks and 65% of the gasworks were municipally owned and operated (Cohn 1910, p. 62). Central to building the foundational infrastructure were not only the 'technical' engineers, but also the 'financial' engineers who (in contrast to present-day financial engineers) worked in support of the same, social objective. While the US pioneered municipal bonds from the early nineteenth century, European municipalities relied on bank lending including that by specialised institutions like the Credit Communal de Belgique founded in 1860. And, of course, some of the savings banks were themselves municipally controlled, such as the Sparkassen in Germany and Austria. Political resistance was overcome because gas and water could generate the revenue from households to repay investment and generate surpluses. The Birmingham model of municipal socialism, invented by Joseph Chamberlain as Mayor in the early 1870s, applied the profits of municipalised gas and water to civic improvement.

As Jane Jacobs (1961, p. 447) put it pithily, the big story of the later nineteenth century is that cities which were 'the most helpless and devastated victims of disease ... became the great disease conquerors'. And everywhere, the driver of change was fear of the water-borne 'zymotic' diseases which killed rich and poor alike. For example, a cholera outbreak in 1830 drove the pioneering extension of the Vienna sewerage system. The last great European cholera outbreak, which killed 10,000 in Hamburg in 1892, was paradoxically caused by contamination of a piped water supply (Evans 1987). But already by this point a different kind of socio-technic innovation was at work at national scale when Bismarck's Germany introduced contributory sickness insurance in 1884 and old age insurance in 1889. As Tilly (1985) argued, the nation state has always been a 'protection racket', which offers security in return for tax revenues; but social insurance allowed the liberal collectivist central state to offer active and positive kinds of protection against the risks that capitalism had created for a new urban, industrial working class.

Contributory social insurance is a way of taxing employers and employees to deal with the inevitable interruptions and insecurities of wage labour in an urban industrial economy. The German and French systems of sickness and old age insurance were prototypical in that they combined old age and sickness insurance, insisted on employer contributions and offered the incentive of state top up. The British resisted contributory old-age pensions but pioneered unemployment insurance cautiously in 1911 as part of the great Liberal reforms sponsored by Lloyd George and Winston Churchill. But the British then went their own way by persevering with a flat-rate system, unlike other European systems that were graduated according to earnings. The achievement of the Beveridge Report in 1942 was to extend that flat-rate system and direct it towards paying a subsistence minimum level of benefit.

Contributory social insurance and its benefits are not in any way inherently the prerogative of the central state at national level. The British National Health Service of 1947 offered free hospitalisation, which had been pioneered at local level with whole population health insurance schemes in two small Welsh industrial towns, Ebbw Vale and Llanelli, in the inter-war period (Webster 2002). Many European systems offered trade unions a part in enrolment, and voluntary organisations a role in delivery. But social insurance was at the leading edge of a kind of Europe-wide nationalisation of the foundational economy in 1945, which increased the role of the central state and greatly diminished that of municipalities.

The nationalisation of the foundational was reinforced by technical changes and organisational preferences in the material sphere, especially in energy and transport, which had hitherto been organised locally and regionally. In electricity, the disrupter was the step change in consumption with the increase in durable usage by networked households, especially in poorer countries with national electrification programmes; in Italy, there was a tenfold increase in electricity production to 200,000 GWh between 1945 and 1985. As electricity consumption levels increased everywhere, larger generating stations were connected to national grids according to central decisions. In France, for example, the first nuclear plant opened in 1962; Prime Minister Pierre Mesmer announced in 1974 the ambition of generating all of France's electricity from nuclear power. The shift from locally produced town gas to pipeline imported natural gas in the 1970s again displaced the possibility of municipal and regional control.

Equally important was the Europe-wide preference after the 1940s for the large, vertically integrated nationalised corporation. This was widely seen as the form of organisation most appropriate for utilities and for state-owned sectors of heavy industry. Command and control organisation could provide top-down planning and distributed technical expertise for nationwide utility systems. It was well adapted to post-1945 frameworks of indicative planning, which in the French case took the form of successive five-year plans. By the 1950s, no

self-respecting European country was complete without a
nationally constructed and managed electricity generating and
distribution system and a nationally organised and owned
railway utility.

But the decisive change in this second period after the Second
World War was the rapid spread, towards nearly universal
coverage, of a wide range of welfare services which were free
or nearly free at-the-point-of-consumption and financed from
taxation of one kind or another. These welfare services were,
therefore, unlike gas and water utilities, which could recover
their costs by billing households for usage on a fixed or variable
basis, or through local taxation, which could add a redistributive element to the citizen's cost of access to the material
foundational economy. The great attraction of social insurance
was that it promised to fund itself, so that a payroll tax on
the working, healthy and young working class would pay for
the unemployed, sick and old. But old-age pensions were an
increasing cost as retirement at 65 was institutionalised and
life expectancy increased, so that years of maintenance allowance had to be paid to a growing cohort of older people. The
extension of income tax to ordinary workers through systems
of weekly pay roll deduction – as under the British Pay-As-
You-Earn System created in the 1940s – was thus an important
and necessary supplementary.

In orthodox terms, the long-term issue was whether 'the
economy' could support the overhead of a providential state's
offering of free welfare services. The transformation of daily
life on an unprecedented scale after 1945 certainly came at a
cost because a greatly expanded providential economy came
with capital and current spending demands on tax revenue,
and this was increased by the requirement to subsidise
utilities like railways when providing cheap inputs for private
users.

This was not a live issue in *Les Trente Glorieuses*, the three
decades after the Second World War, when the conjuncture was
benign and the economy appeared manageable for sustained

growth and productivity increase. Keynesian economic policies, with or without national corporatist bargaining, aimed for historically high economic growth rates and full employment. This was more or less achieved, as long as a 'Fordist' system of industrial production and consumption sustained a large working class employed in historically highly paid jobs in manufacturing industry. In context, at this time, most large European countries produced three quarters or more of their manufactures domestically and exported the rest to a grateful world without fear of low-wage competition.

But this was an inherently precarious phase of global development in recovery from world war and 1930s autarchy. It was not a semi-permanent achievement resting on coherent national conditions. Since material and providential provision were so closely bound up with Keynesianism and its associated industrial economy, it followed that the two domains of the material and providential would suffer collateral damage if the systems of economic government and industrial production were damaged. This is exactly what happened from the early 1970s.

The damage to Keynesian economic management was benchmarked by the two great oil shocks of 1972–4 and 1979–81, their associated recessions and the onset of a toxic combination of stagnant growth and inflation – stagflation – across most advanced capitalist economies. These economic problems sucked the life out of the philosophies that had underlain the historically established foundational economy – notably those that had assumed the technical superiority of professionally managed systems of public administration and the collectivist necessity of delivering free or heavily subsidised services. From the early 1980s onwards the most vibrant public philosophies were neoliberal in character, and states increasingly shifted policies into a frame of making 'the economy' work by tax cuts and marketisation.

An associated set of problems afflicted the system of industrial production on which both Keynesianism and the providential domain of the foundational economy were based. The end of *Les Trente Glorieuses* in the early 1970s coincided with a renewed burst of globalisation. The giant centres of industrial employment were increasingly eviscerated, as production was, to a growing extent, organised around global supply chains where companies sought the cheapest location for labour. The age of high-paid 'Fordist' employment that had created a well-paid working class which could contribute its taxes to the support of the foundational economy, came to an end.

Under these conditions, centralised national power (which had been constructive in expanding the providential and nationalising the material in the decades after the 1940s) became destructive through privatisation, outsourcing and service cuts after the early 1980s. The sidelining of municipal or regional centres of decision making and the marginalisation of intermediary institutions and not-for-profit organisations was all represented in the first period after 1945, as the economic precondition of effective management control of the foundational; in the next period after 1980 the absence of independent regional centres and autonomous institutions turned out to be the political precondition of privatisation and outsourcing because it undermined the possibility of political resistance to this preying on the foundational economy. Change in central policy empowered new forces – in financial markets and in corporate business – as a powerful lobby arguing for the admission of fund investors and private corporates that promised reorganisation of service delivery for the benefit of 'customers'.

All this played out differently across Europe. The British are discontented because of what Margaret Thatcher and Tony Blair did in their extraordinarily centralised polity now soured by years of austerity cuts; the French and Italians are discontented because their polities have long blocked the kinds of Blairite reforms that figures like Matteo Renzi and Emmanuel Macron advocate; the Germans back up half-hearted reform with a huge surplus from export success under the euro regime, which has dire costs in Southern Europe, especially Greece. In some countries, resistance to the undermining of foundational provision arises from resilient federal structures and municipal autonomy, which have acted as a stabiliser against more general pressures from neoliberalism and corporatisation. After noting these various outcomes, we would say that our next aim is not to write a history of divergent outcomes but to understand how and why the projects of privatisation and outsourcing preyed on an increasingly disorganised foundational economy. This is the theme of our next chapter.

Appendix 2.1: Activities classified as material, providential or overlooked

Material foundational economy: the pipes and cables, networks and branches which continuously connect households to daily essentials; now often privatised.

- Pipe and cable utilities add electricity, gas, water sewerage and telecoms, now including broadband. Transportation/ mobility systems include infrastructure and vehicles i.e. railways, roads, filling stations and all the public/social vehicles such as trains and buses. The universal postal delivery service but not private couriers like DHL.
- We would include food (production, processing and distribu- tion) because purchase is frequent, necessary and heavily dependent on infrastructure to bring it close to households. Access to banking services and the payments system is also essential to everyday life and, therefore, we include retail banking.
- We have included car retailing and servicing, but not car manufacture because cars are often used for basic mobility with no alternative in many rural or urban areas with limited public transport.

Providential foundational economy: a subset of (mainly) public-sector welfare activity providing the universal services available to all citizens; now increasingly outsourced.

- Health, education, social care, police and prisons/law and order, funerals, public administration. Plus their close and exclusive private suppliers but not the whole private supply chains, for example, dispensing chemists which support healthcare, but not pharmaceutical companies.
- Housing was excluded from our original foundational employment calculations (and we now put housing construction employment in the overlooked). There is, in practice, a contest between social housing as right and private housing as asset, with the line between social right and household asset changing between countries and over time.

Overlooked economy: goods and services culturally defined as essential and requiring occasional purchase, for example, the sofa for your house, holiday from work etc.

- A variety of everyday necessities which: a) present as mundane and are taken for granted occasional purchases through a variety of channels and come in a cultural wrapper of style; and b) lifestyle support goods and services which can be often low-tech goods or mundane support services: for example, clothing, furniture including beds and sofas, double glazing and central heating or air conditioning, house maintenance, body maintenance including hairdressing, pet food and vet services, leisure including tourism, hospitality and airports.
- This is a changing socio-culturally defined list, for example, central heating in UK houses only became a mundane necessity in the 1970s, and air conditioning in Australia in the 1980s.

Notes

1 www.gov.za/speeches/dws-acknowledges-findings-statssa-water-and-sanitation-provision-3-jun-2016-0000 (accessed 8 February 2018).

2 www.statssa.gov.za/?p=9145 (accessed 8 February 2018).

3 https://washdata.org/data#!/zaf (accessed 8 February 2018).

4 www.eskom.co.za/news/Pages/Dec7.aspx (accessed 8 February 2018).

5 http://thebrazilbusiness.com/article/stealing-infrastructure-access-in-brazil (accessed 8 February 2018).

6 https://www.economist.com/news/middle-east-and-africa/21713858-why-it-bottom-class-south-africa-has-one-worlds-worst-education (accessed 8 February 2018).

7 https://www.huffingtonpost.com/salim-lamrani/cubas-health-care-system-_b_5649968.html (accessed 8 February 2018).

8 See, for example: Christophers (2011) on the finance sector; Waring (1990) for a classic feminist critique of GDP; and Stiglitz, Sen and Fitoussi (2009) for a general evaluation.

9 For example, in the UK, the Joseph Rowntree Foundation has published analysis of 'inverse care' using the 2001 census data. This shows how provision of skilled staff in public services and other resources can often vary inversely with local levels of poverty. Available at: https://www.jrf.org.uk/report/relationship-between-poverty-affluence-and-area. For the Bhutan experiment see https://www.theguardian.com/world/2012/dec/01/bhutan-wealth-happiness-counts (accessed 8 February 2018).

10 Source at: http://ec.europa.eu/eurostat/web/science-technology-innovation/data/database (accessed 8 February 2018).

11 http://hansard.parliament.uk/Commons/2017-01-11/debates/2A2F4EA1-3973-49A0-809-3B00B7756994/NHSAndSocialCareFunding#contribution-5DAE2BDC-7CCD-4DE7-BDCD-8788EA87F065 (accessed 8 February 2018).

12 See: https://www.thebalance.com/largest-retail-grocery-stores-3862931 (accessed 8 February 2018).

13 NACE is the EU system of industry/economic activity classification (from the French term *nomenclature statistique des activités économiques dans la Communauté européenne*; SIC stands for standard industry classification, as used in the UK.

14 foundationaleconomy.com is a website that provides access to academic research, public interest reports and other items, contributed by the authors of this book and a wider group of international researchers.

15 For more information on the UK, see the website of Shelter: http://england.shelter.org.uk/campaigns_/why_we_campaign/ housing_facts_and_figures/subsection?section=housing_ supply#hf_5 (accessed 8 February 2018); or www. historyandpolicy.org/policy-papers/papers/the-right-to-buy-history-and-prospect (accessed 8 February 2018).

16 For example, on the development of water and sewerage in European cities, see Jutti and Katko (2005); on public and social services in European countries, see Wollmann (2016).

3   Wrecking the foundational

Follow the money

> The rail industry in Great Britain was liberalised in the mid-1990s ... [O]ver the past 20 years, the number of passenger journeys have more than doubled ... Growth has been accompanied by a strong safety record second only to Ireland ... In a European comparison, Great Britain comes second after Finland in terms of passenger satisfaction which stood at just below 80% ... GB rail has comparable punctuality performance with other European railways ... The UK has delivered operating costs below the European average, performing better than France (second highest), Belgium, the Netherlands and Austria ... The UK has responded to growth in the passenger and freight demand by investing more than any other Member State in rail. (Wright and Besslich 2017)

The UK rail system was privatised in the mid-1990s when the state-owned British Rail corporation was broken up. Twenty years later, the Rail Delivery Group is the trade association bringing together all the providers in the UK's system, including franchised train operators and train leasing companies. In the above quotation, the Rail Delivery Group poses the rhetorical question, 'What makes Britain's railways great?' And it supplies an answer by listing many good things delivered, and by presenting a series of comparisons between high-performing 'liberalised' British railways and under-performing mainland European railways. The implication is that in earlier times the British were, as other countries still are, held back by the dead hand of public ownership and the absence of the kind of internal competition now being promoted by the EU.

This kind of passage is typical of the narratives put together by privatised or outsourced providers of foundational services. They never include any costs, preferring to just add up the many benefits which are all attributed to the sole cause of private ownership or operation. Researchers working on rail could and should challenge the claims point by point, as we have done in a public interest report when telling a different story (Bowman *et al.* 2013a). Under state ownership by the early 1990s the British rail network already had lower operating costs than mainland peers; the increase in passenger numbers since privatisation owes more to GDP growth and London house prices than rail company marketing; capital investment in the privatised system was effectively state financed, and the resulting debt of more than £40 billion now sits on the government's balance sheet.

But it is also necessary to produce a broader narrative, which goes beyond refuting trade claims which are half-truths and de-contextualised misinformation. This narrative should present an analysis of the wrecking of the foundational economy: specifically, how and why things go wrong after privatisation, corporatisation, outsourcing and other forms of 'restructuring'. These actions collectively represent a financial re-engineering of the foundational, which inserts new claims and priorities, while also reorganising and undermining these social and material infrastructures. For this purpose, we turn to 'follow-the-money' analysis. In popular usage, 'follow the money' is narrowly associated with the uncovering of law-breaking and crime. In the 1976 *Watergate* movie, Deep Throat tells the *Washington Post* reporter to 'follow the money' if he wants to understand the break-in; more recently, *Follow the Money* is the (translated) title of a 'Scandi Noir' TV series about false accounting at a green energy company. But beyond these popular fictions there is a more serious purpose: follow-the-money methods can be applied to understand the predatory but entirely legal operations of financialised capitalism.

It is not easy to do this kind of follow-the-money research. It requires more than a basic knowledge of accounting categories like the distinction between profit and cash, and the ability to read a balance sheet. The accounting numbers must be related to financial market return requirements and product market margin possibilities. This context then provides an understanding of what business models must and can do to deliver in financial terms; and about how, in delivering financial results, these business models reward or punish different stakeholders. Financial engineering now adds many complications when large corporates and fund investors have morphed into groups using tiers of interconnected companies, in different jurisdictions (including tax havens with limited disclosure). In 2015, for instance, the Four Seasons group of around 400 UK care homes consisted of 185 companies in more than 10 tiers across six jurisdictions, including the Isle of Man, Guernsey, Jersey, Barbados and the Cayman Islands (Burns *et al.* 2016, p. 38).

Leaks from law firms inside tax havens, like the Panama and Paradise Papers, rightly make for sensational revelations on the front pages of newspapers across Europe.[1] The revelations are about complicated inter-company transactions involving sales of assets and intra-group debt at above market rates, designed to shift profits between jurisdictions and minimise tax liabilities. But this chapter presents a follow-the-money account which is differently focused because it does not put secrecy and tax havens at the centre of the story. Our follow-the-money account uses publicly available sources (not leaks) about the everyday operating systems of financialised capitalism (mainly) within European jurisdictions. The story here is not only about the devices of financial engineering levered on the use of debt and tax shelters within (and without) the home jurisdiction; it is also about the financial benefits obtained by private operators from the use of power against other stakeholders.

It is important not to demonise the companies and fund investors who are doing all this. They can plead diminished responsibility because their behaviours are driven by the requirements of the financial markets which are institutionalised in their business models. Since the innovation of high-yield bonds in the 1980s and the growth of asset allocation to private equity, expectations of return have been raised. Stock market quoted companies just as much as private equity funds cannot now be content with the 5% returns on capital, which was the norm for shareholders in railway companies and holders of government bonds in the late nineteenth century, when the material infrastructure of the foundational economy was being built. And these issues about expectations of higher returns are therefore relevant not only to newly privatised or outsourced activities but to other institutions – like supermarkets and retail banks – which have long been privately held, but since the 1990s have been under pressure to deliver (more) shareholder value, which means higher returns on capital, preferably with growth of earnings and profit.

Under financial market pressure, the result is a kind of predation which is peculiar to financialised capitalism – a system which is run by self-serving elites directing institutions that are increasingly careless of any social responsibility. In countries like South Africa or Saudi Arabia we have pillaging and looting via elite commissions on private deals and revenue skimming on public projects, which is tolerated by government but undermines institutions and rule of law. In financialised Northern Europe, we have proceduralised predation on the advice of the best lawyers and accountants that money can buy. Corporate elites are enriched by remuneration committee or fee structure as they preside over formal restructurings and initiatives for higher returns as well as daily opportunism against weaker stakeholders like workforce or suppliers; all this is enabled by governments which lament private sector excesses but appear to have no alternatives to shareholder value and a bias against direct state provision. While the UK is often considered the natural European home of privatisation and outsourcing, the reorganisation of public services by bringing in private interests is actually most advanced in Sweden (Milne 2016).

The second and third sections of this chapter present a follow-the-money analysis of predation and how, in foundational activities, levered power and financial engineering fit together into business models which work through exploitation and extraction. These points are illustrated using British and Italian case material on foundational activities so that we can build the argument that sectoral dynamics vary and national economies are different, but the usual outcome is disorganisation and disembedding of the foundational firms and sectors. A new financialised economy has been organised since the 1980s around the principle of point value, short time horizons and cash extraction for investors; this point value approach is particularly ill suited to foundational activities which generate a modest long run, stream of value for citizens, continuously over a period of time. Before turning to these themes, the first section below analyses the political and economic drivers which explain how and why so much of the foundational economy was carelessly and complacently privatised and outsourced in the thirty years after 1980.

Careless privatisation and outsourcing

We saw in Chapter 2 that the construction of the foundational economy was a century-long achievement, but it was an achievement that was often invisible and thus taken for granted. In 1980, when the age of privatisation and outsourcing was beginning, almost nobody had a clear concept of the foundational or a vision of the way its material elements provided the infrastructure of civilised life. Prevailing official and academic concepts of national income and the welfare state were part of a division of labour between economics and sociology which tended to make the foundational economy invisible. In the economy, as in personal life, if we cannot name or otherwise recognise something, we are unlikely to value it. So it was, then, that right across Europe, large parts of the publicly constructed and operated foundational economy were privatised, outsourced or otherwise restructured in the thirty years after 1980 in a process which was carelessly driven by politicians and complacently sanctioned by mainstream economists. This process of privatisation was initially prompted by changing attitudes towards public debt and taxation, but it became increasingly bound up with the state's inability to finance foundational infrastructure and services, something that became an acute problem after the great financial crisis of 2007–9.

The prototype of all this was Thatcherism in the UK, and Margaret Thatcher's speeches are illuminating on the political preconditions of privatisation. She had no clear vision of how privatisation would bring unspecified 'efficiencies' but offered many rhetorical listings of the manifest costs of public ownership: 'the public ceases to have any ownership or accountability … [but] starts to pay. Pays to take the industry over. Pays the losses by higher taxes. Pays for inefficiencies in higher prices' (Thatcher 1976). In this characteristic and often repeated account, public ownership is equated with failed state socialism, and privatisation as the necessary free market corrective (with the earlier municipal socialism of centrist parties nowhere in sight). Thus, from the late 1980s, 'privatise and outsource' had the same axiomatic status for neoliberal ideologues as Snowball's slogan in George Orwell's *Animal Farm*, 'four legs good two legs bad'.

Across Europe, policy ideals shift between panaceas in a fashion cycle lasting about thirty years. Since 1945, the syllogism which justifies every major policy regime change is that if strategy (a) is a dismal failure, then the opposite strategy (b) will deliver policy objectives. The antidote fallacy gave us nationalisation and the state-owned corporation after 1945 as the antidote to dysfunctional private owners; then, from the early 1980s, gave us privatisation and outsourcing as the antidote to bureaucratic public corporations and state employment. Some thirty years later we are at a point where the cycle of policy fashion means that re-nationalisation and remunicipalisation once again has political traction in the UK and beyond, with a broader resistance elsewhere to unfettered private interests in public services (Aralal and Wu 2010).

The causes of failed public ownership strategy (a) were always blurred in the 1980s. The prejudice against the integrated state-owned corporation or direct state employment always rested on the assumption that the public sector's problem was labour control and high input costs. This ignored the possibility that Europe's nationalised heavy industries had charged low output prices, effectively subsidising other (mainly private) sectors. It also ignored the possibility that integrated, engineering-led organisations were best suited to running technically complex networks. The definition of privatisation strategy (b) after the early 1980s was rhetorical and imaginary. That is, it offered an ideal to contrast with the reality of nationalisation. In arguing against public ownership of rail networks, for example, advocates of privatisation consistently failed to engage with activity specifics, including the problem that, in most European railway networks (with or without public ownership and regardless of fares policy), there has never been enough money from fares to cover operating costs *and* capital investment.

Because many politicians default into thinking in Manichean categories without engaging specifics, civil servants and technical experts who negotiate complexities should then be an important safeguard in any democratic polity. Unfortunately, the processes of privatisation and outsourcing were not carefully scrutinised but carelessly legitimated by experts after the early

1980s. As we can see in the UK, the underlying problem here was not experts but the outsourcing of public policy and decision making to the wrong kind of experts: investment bankers, business service consultants and think tanks with mainstream economists providing the intellectual support. Investment banks and the big accountancy and consulting firms lived in a transactional and contractual world; they could not be expected to understand the value of integrated organisation and in-house expertise. The think tanks that clustered around College Green outside the Houses of Parliament produced retail policy, ready for today or tomorrow's announcements; their role was therefore not to challenge but to accommodate or press further the received wisdom and assumptions of politicians. As for academic social scientists, they were divided into multiple factions and, on privatisation and outsourcing, it was the mainstream economists who had the influence because they were numerous, shared common beliefs and were not handicapped by self-doubt.

Mainstream economists after the mid-1980s believed that they had developed new techniques of regulation which could be applied to manage privately owned foundational utilities in the interests of consumers. This undermined the technocratic bias for public ownership in such activities because economists had traditionally characterised these utilities as 'natural monopolies', where private operators could improve margins by raising prices to exploit the consumer. From the 1983 Littlechild report onwards in the UK, economists developed a new model of regulation by independent agency, initially in telecoms, and later exported it to other sectors and OECD countries (Littlechild 1983, 1986.) The new model had two key elements: first, the regulatory agency should actively promote competition in utility markets or alternatively sponsor competition for the market through service franchising; and, second, the regulatory agency should introduce forward-looking regulation with mandated investment requirements and efficiency gains, classically by setting prices through an inflation-related formula like RPI minus 1 (the formula that claimed to squeeze out efficiencies by suppressing price increase systematically to one percentage point below the rate of price inflation, the retail price index, RPI).

Foundational utility regulation was thereby defined as an adjunct to orthodox anti-trust, competition and markets policy. This already existed in all EU countries, having been enshrined in 1957 in the founding Treaty of Rome. Article 101 of the Treaty prohibited cartel agreements between two or more independent market operators which restrict competition; article 102 prohibited a firm with a dominant market position from charging unfair prices or limiting production. Within this larger frame, new model regulation of privatised utilities promised to make natural monopoly socially responsible by weakening dominant market positions or simulating the effects of competition.

All this rested on a kind of category mistake between the characteristics of an abstract textbook model of capitalism and the behaviour of actual capitalists after financialisation. The authors of the new model regulation were promoting an abstract model of capitalism where competition and markets drive benefits for consumers. Actual capitalists (corporate managers and fund investors) by contrast, have always preferred profits from the abridgement of competition. And if that was blocked by competition policy, they now operated in a financialised world where profits on capital and cash extraction are crucial and can be secured, as we shall see in the next section, by the use of power against other stakeholders and by the devices of financial engineering which utility regulation never considered.

This confusion about the object of regulation was bound to end badly for the rest of us because the economists as regulators were watching prices and investment while the managers and fund investors were manipulating cash extraction. The results were quite surreal in the case of UK water and sewerage, which was privatised in 1989 under the regulatory agency Ofwat.[2]

The regulator used five-yearly reviews to fix prices according to the 'K factor', which in this case is RPI plus a set margin to cover investment. Within this frame, the operators have been allowed to distribute all their post-tax profits as dividends; in the decade to 2016, £18.1 billion was distributed out of total profits of £18.8 billion. The problem was then to finance investment with no retained earnings. This was solved initially by charging consumers for water clean-up through the pricing formula, and then by operator borrowing so that sector debt rose from almost zero in 1989 to nearly £40 billion in 2016 (Baylis and Hall 2017). Under irrelevant regulation, the operators were effectively allowed to finance cash extraction now by piling up debt liabilities in the future; and all of this debt was private-sector borrowing at much higher rates than the state would have paid.

The sale and franchising of foundational services bears some resemblance to two earlier historical episodes, involving the sale of staple monopolies by early modern European monarchs. Charles I in England after 1629 sold staple and semi-luxury monopolies like salt, soap and currants; while Louis XIV in France after 1688 sold not just offices but the right to perform commercial functions. The sole driver here was financial embarrassment, which made it attractive to create capital value out of established sources of state income: Charles' sale of staple monopolies in the 1630s was simply 'the line of least resistance' when Parliament would not vote tax revenues as income for the king (McColvin 2012, p. 34; Hill 1961, p. 35).

But the modern story is more complicated because it is about more than the fiscal crisis of a state. It intersects with changing central state attitudes towards public debt and unacknowledged reliance on private debt; outside Southern Europe, the problem of EU states reaching the limits of their borrowing power was much less of a constraint than in the early modern period, and this was so even after 2010 in the period of austerity. Attitudes and constraints worked together in EU countries to shift the availability of publicly borrowed capital and tax revenue funding. The end result was two-fold: first, from the 1980s, a squeeze on capital funding for foundational activities whose investment had traditionally been publicly funded; second, after the great financial crisis of 2007–9, a squeeze on revenue funding for foundational services in activities like health and social care.

The publicly acknowledged story here starts with defeats for the organised working class – a key part of the coalition that in the thirty years after the Second World War had supported the material and the providential foundational economy. Through wage bargaining, by the 1970s unionised workers were able to claim a high share of national income and compensation for rising prices; as a result, organised labour was taking the blame for inflation which hurt asset holders. That rationalised the introduction of monetarist policies to curb inflation and Anglo-American political confrontations like Reagan's defeat of the air traffic controllers in 1981 or Thatcher's struggle with the miners in 1984–5. After these defeats, a clampdown on public investment and tax-funded public services had a kind of perverse logic and (for different reasons in various countries) workers did not receive enhancements in the form of tax-funded public services and investment in foundational welfare, to help offset what they had been denied in wage bargaining. In non-Anglo-Saxon countries, the transition to neoliberal priorities was more blurred. For example, in Italy, the workers' movement suffered a historical defeat in Turin Fiat plants in 1980, after a 35-day strike. But in a country where the two main mass-parties were Christian Democrat and Communist, political initiative in privatisation and other public reforms then became the responsibility of technocrats (not ideologically motivated right and centrist politicians).

While purposive structural reform was in the public domain and on the front pages of newspapers, the undisclosed and unintended consequences of financialisation drove growth in the European national economies after the mid-1980s. More precisely, the deregulation of finance, symbolised by the Big Bang changes of 1986 in London Stock Exchange rules, inaugurated a new capitalist regime. This liberalisation not only institutionalised the higher return requirements for non-financial firms, already implicit in US high-yield bonds and leveraged private equity funds. It also unleashed finance for itself within investment banking, as unregulated credit creation allowed financial firms to create a superstructure of new classes of financial assets, like derivatives, on a basis of cheap credit for ordinary households. Ordinary households were intricated in this financialisation on an unprecedented mass scale; household pension contributions and insurance premia provided the feedstock for funds seeking higher returns (whose net benefits for pensioners were limited by intermediary deductions); while house property became an appreciating asset when credit creation was facilitated by the innovation of securitisation which allowed issuers to sell on mortgage loans.

The result before (and after) the 2007–9 financial crisis was 'privatised Keynesianism' (Crouch 2009), with private consumption boosted on the upswing by cash withdrawal after re-mortgage of a house or flat whose market price had increased. This had the effect of creating a bias against the foundational economy because households were taking out more private debt to supplement wages and fund individual consumption. The UK provides the classic case. Here, more than 60% of GDP was private consumption demand, and increases in GDP were largely dependent on leakage into current private consumption in two successive booms as householders re-mortgaged against rising house prices. In the UK case, as Exhibit 3.1 shows, housing equity withdrawal was larger than nominal GDP growth under both Prime Ministers Margaret Thatcher and Tony Blair. Housing became the dominant

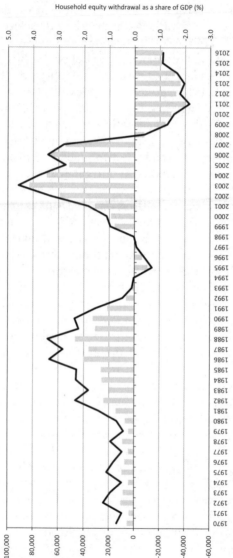

Exhibit 3.1 Total UK equity withdrawal and as a share of UK GDP (%)
(Equity withdrawal relates to sterling withdrawals and is in 2016 prices)
Source: Bank of England and ONS

pro-cyclical force on the upswings in both premierships (and, predictably, worked in the opposite direction after the post-2008 downswing).

The long-term consequence of relying on private debt to boost consumption and a bias against the foundational was that peculiarly Anglo-American combination of private affluence and public squalor, which citizens feel and see as they drive over ill-surfaced roads or pass neglected public parks. The UK and US were, admittedly, outlier cases. In both the UK and US in 2006 just before the crisis, the value of outstanding mortgages was equivalent to more than 100% of disposable income, whereas in Germany and Italy it was 71% and 39% respectively. Here, as in so much to do with financialisation, the British and Americans led the way to a new kind of rentier capitalism.

The term rentier capitalism is loosely used to denote the many different forms of capitalism where rents from holding financial assets or property supplement incomes earned from making and selling manufactured goods or services. The new EU form of rentier capitalism after the 1980s had two central characteristics. First, large corporates and fund investors diverted from raising and allocating capital to extracting higher returns on capital; the result in the foundational economy was financial engineering and levered use of power against stakeholders, as described in the next section. Second, half the households everywhere (except in Germany) were offered unearned income through rising house prices; the result was inherent macroeconomic instability. This instability was increasingly compounded by economic management which increasingly bought GDP growth by making private credit cheap and readily available, as with post-2008 monetary policies.

Matters were further complicated by changing attitudes to public expenditure. In a parallel process, foundational provision was directly threatened by tighter limits on borrowing after the 1970s in countries where public debt was growing amidst increasing difficulty in raising tax revenue to cover current expenditure. In Streeck's (2015) account, the 'debt state' was created in OECD countries after the 1970s: as the tax share of GDP peaked, inflation subsided, growth rates slowed and unemployment increased. In support, Streeck cites a 30-point increase to 75% in the OECD average of government debt to GDP in the twenty years after the first oil shock. If that is correct, we would note that the OECD average also covers divergent national trends and variable constraints. After the early 1990s, the Italian ratio of debt to GDP is never below 100% and the French ratio climbs inexorably to that level, while the UK and Germany contain government debt to GDP in the range 35–65% before 2007.

At least before the great financial crisis in 2007, the general European problem was not primarily a structural problem about indebted states meeting absolute limits on borrowing. The problem was more an ideational problem in finance ministries across Europe with the spread of a 'can't pay, won't pay' attitude towards public funding of renewal investment in foundational infrastructure. Responsibility for infrastructure finance could then be passed onto the financial markets via privatisation. This was clearest in the UK, where the pioneering privatisation of the British Telecom utility in 1984 was driven, in large measure, by the Treasury's reluctance to pay for a programme of investment in electronic replacements for Strowger mechanical exchanges (Bowman *et al.* 2014, p. 35). The classic UK privatisations of water and energy in the late 1980s were pressed through as the UK ratio of debt to GDP fell to an all-time low of 32% in 1992 with the overall level below 50% for thirty-five years after the early 1970s. The proceeds of UK privatisation sales were not needed to plug budget deficits; indeed, in some cases revenue raising was very much a secondary concern and assets were deliberately under-priced (Grout, Jenkins and Zalewska 2001).

Everything changed in the financial crisis after 2008. It led to hugely increased public debt and unbalanced budgets, which gave teeth to EU rules about limits on current budget deficits. Politicians and central bankers saved the banks in the crisis and afterwards then relied on experimental monetary stimulus. This caused a spike increase in the public debt to GDP ratio, which has since been reduced only in Germany. In the UK case, the total of public debt jumped up towards 80% of GDP and the current annual budget deficit increased alarmingly from £20 to £100 billion, reaching nearly 7% of GDP in 2010 (Exhibit 3.2). In these circumstances, austerity cuts in tax revenue that funded foundational services were legitimated as necessary to avoid fiscal deficits and reduce public debt. The question was not whether to cut, but how deep and sustained the cuts in foundational provision should be; the misery was inevitably prolonged insofar as national economic models were now built on private debt and deregulated labour markets.

The financial crisis in many ways just brought forward inherent problems about the pursuit of growth and jobs through such means: private debt stimulates erratic, unsustainable growth of GDP; low-wage jobs increase demands for providential spending on income support. Privatised Keynesianism became a recipe for boom-and-bust economic growth because house prices cannot rise indefinitely, and corrections of uncertain severity and duration are inevitable. After 2008, there was a nasty bust in house prices in many European countries; ten years later house prices have not recovered to pre-crisis levels in Denmark, Greece, Ireland and Spain; while house price increases of more than 50% in Austria, Norway and Sweden feed debt-based private consumption. Further instabilities were added when in the UK case the labour market was deregulated in the American way. In the British version this American-style deregulation was combined with some providential safeguards in the European style of income support for the low paid. This spread low-wage employment and increased demands for various kinds of wage subsidy. In the UK case, as Exhibit 3.3 shows, the number of dependent

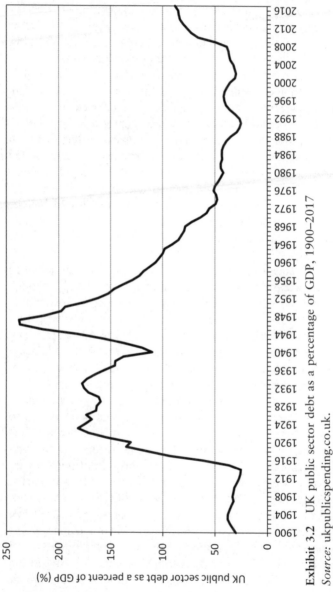

Exhibit 3.2 UK public sector debt as a percentage of GDP, 1900–2017

Source: ukpublicspending.co.uk.

https://www.ukpublicspending.co.uk/
spending_chart_1900_2017UKp_17c1li111tcn_G0t_UK_National_Debt_since_1900.

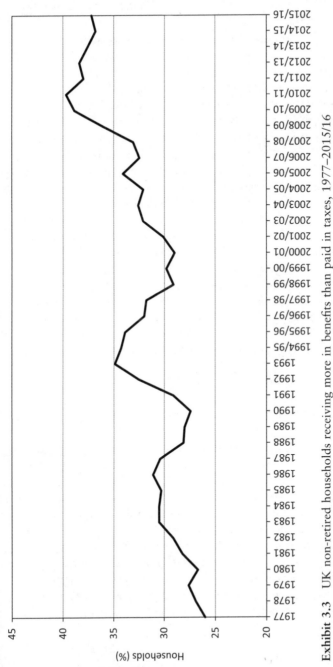

Exhibit 3.3 UK non-retired households receiving more in benefits than paid in taxes, 1977–2015/16

Note: 'Benefits' include both cash benefits (such as the state pension, housing benefit and tax credits) and benefits in kind (such as education and the NHS). 'Taxes' include direct and indirect taxes.

Source: ONS, https://www.ons.gov.uk/peoplepopulationandcommunity/personalandhouseholdfinances/incomeandwealth/adhocs/006977numberandpercentageofhouseholdsreceivingmoreinbenefitsthanpaidintaxes1977tofinancialyearending2016.

working households receiving more in benefits than they paid in taxes increased from 27% to nearly 40% between 1979 and 2010; subsequent austerity cuts in state benefits have not reduced this key percentage by more than 2–3%.

This history of the privatised and outsourced foundational economy since the 1908s is therefore a story of the modern sale of the monopolies against a background of careless thought and undisclosed policy objectives. The developing aversion to public investment in the services of the foundational economy was paralleled by the development of a privatised Keynesian consumption system that depended on the sugar rush of income from privately held assets, notably property. The logic of all this was intensified by the policy response to the great financial crisis which degraded public finances in a way that licensed a new age of austerity. This was disastrous for providential services dependent on continuing revenue funding. But the foundational was also struggling, even before the age of austerity, with the toxic consequences of privatisation and outsourcing in a financialised system, as levered power plus financial engineering led to predation. That is what we examine in the next part of this chapter.

Levered power and the devices of financial engineering

If we were asked to play an association game with the word 'business', it would bring out positives and negatives: yes, business is innovative, hard-working, employment creating, and delivers useful goods and services; but business can also be extractive, imitative, abusive of stakeholders and deceitful. When business is both, the eternal issue is how we get more of the good business and less of the bad. The practical issue in our own time is why we have so much bad business, like retail banks which mis-sell financial products, car companies which have gamed the EU diesel emission businesses and debt laden fragile corporate chains in adult and child care?

Since the 1970s we have thoroughly confused these issues through rhetoric which represents all business as 'enterprise', and through a narrow economics which relates the difference between good and bad business monomaniacally to the presence or absence of competitive markets and producers with market power. Against this, we argue that (while monopoly is seldom beneficial) the drivers of business behaviour are much more complex and it is essential to consider activity specifics. This point about specifics is crucial if we are trying to explain why financialised providers in the foundational economy routinely rely on financial engineering devices or the use of levered power against other stakeholders.

Most foundational activities (like delivering water or rail transport) have physical characteristics that make them low risk, long time horizon activities where, historically, public and private providers of investment funds have accepted modest, steady financial returns. But privatisation and outsourcing, in a financialised world, brought in public companies and private equity under pressure from the financial markets for substantially higher returns. This section explains how higher returns on capital can be extracted from foundational activities in two ways: first, by the use of power to lever returns up at the expense of other stakeholders like workers or suppliers or customers; second, by the use of financial engineering devices which are levered on capital itself through arbitrage of accounting rules and tax regulations, or on stakeholders like employees or society at large.

Any discussion of this subject should start by considering the question of foundational activity characteristics, risks and returns. The foundational economy, as we saw in Chapter 2, was transformed in the century after 1880. It was governed by its own long cycles of step-change innovation, very different from the short term horizons characteristic of modern shareholder-driven enterprises. On the supply side, in physical infrastructure, the reservoirs built in the thirty years before 1914 are still supplying Europe's cities; and we all use nineteenth-century railway stations and wait for trains on many of the same platforms as our great grandparents. The demand side likewise runs according to long cycles: for instance, the growing number of older people requiring state-funded care can be reliably predicted by simple, intelligible models of an ageing population. Demand for care will not vary cyclically, nor will it unexpectedly fall away like the demand for many consumer products.

The other important point is that the foundational is, to adopt Frank Knight's terminology, a domain of uncertainty, not statistically calculable risk which can be priced in the financial markets. Typically, with foundational infrastructure, a lumpy initial investment earns modest steady returns, until at some unpredictable point in the future, another step-change innovation renders the infrastructure worthless (or maybe part reusable as with copper wire in broadband systems). This point is most obvious in health and social care, where the driver is changing social views about the appropriateness of institutional treatment away from home and community. For example, in France and England, the nineteenth century state innovated by creating national systems of asylums for the mentally ill; but from the mid-twentieth century the large asylums were closed so that mental illness could be treated in the community, or in smaller institutions on a more domestic scale.

All these points about foundational risk and return are statements of the obvious but they provide an essential context for understanding the impact of new privatised and outsourced providers in foundational activities. Stock market quoted corporate players, private equity houses and fund investors approached foundational activities without recognising that these were not high risk/high return/short time horizon activities. Their expectations of high risk and high return were, as we have argued, driven by financial innovation around asset allocation, reinforced from the early 1990s by shareholder value ideology and finance theory that dictated the need for a premium over risk-free returns. These players had equity and debt funding of various kinds and different approaches as to how they would mix cash from profitable operating businesses with gains from buying and selling businesses or business assets. But all aimed for returns on capital of 10% or more – with returns preferably supplemented by growth (organic or via acquisitions) to boost profits and capital values.

In contemporary financialised capitalism, the normalised expectation is for a 10% or more return on capital employed (ROCE), preferably with the bonus of growth of earnings and/or capital value.[3] Since the advent of shareholder value in the early 1990s, the return is an institutionalised requirement which applies to long-established private foundational institutions like stock market quoted retail banks as much as to newly privatised operators. It is enforced by the pressure to deliver shareholder value on the stock market and by the requirement in private equity to make a surplus over what is paid to the bondholders on leveraged transactions which are financed mainly by selling bonds to third parties (Froud *et al.* 2006). Corporate chief executive officers and chief financial officers, who deliver what is considered to be an inadequate return on capital in public companies, must fear for their jobs; sectors that consistently deliver less may over time have to leave the stock market. Similarly, general partners in private equity houses with mediocre returns will find it very difficult to raise another fund and, at current interest rates, may see investee companies pass into the hands of their bond holders if overall returns fall to 7% or lower.

But foundational infrastructure had classically been built by central or local government which paid 5% or less on their borrowings; shareholders in privately owned foundational businesses like nineteenth-century railway companies had accepted similar returns.

- Solvent European governments could for most of the nineteenth century borrow at interest rates below 5%:

British Government Consols were the benchmark risk-free investment and they typically yielded just over 3%. With central bank interest rates currently near zero, solvent European governments are able to borrow for less. Since 2008, the yield on triple A euro area government bonds (the price of long-term public borrowing) has been below 5%, and since autumn 2014 below 2%.

• In privately owned nineteenth-century railway companies, 5% was the norm. Some mineral lines paid handsome dividends and the social returns on the transport services provided by railway companies were high, but overall returns to British railway shareholders were never much over 5%; indeed, they fell below that level in the 1890s and never recovered (Mitchell, Chambers and Crafts 2009.)

When the private sector moved further into the foundational economy after 1990, there was therefore an expectations gap. The foundational economy had historically been built around a norm of 5% returns; the new privatised operators had expectations of 10% returns, which they could not easily adjust downwards. So the service operator's problem was how to extract high returns from foundational activities. The solutions to that problem, we will now see, raise large questions about the bad business consequent upon management action to raise returns.

The difference between 5% and 10% is large in capital intensive activities. This shift could be achieved by doubling of the surplus but that increase in the numerator would require significantly higher prices and/or lower costs, even where it might also be possible to reduce the denominator of the capital base. In practice, attempts to meet rate of return expectations have generally meant hitting on stakeholders for cost reduction through reductions in the wages paid to labour or in the prices paid to suppliers. Looking at the problem another way, if and when returns of 10% plus have been normalised, a halving of the cost of capital would usually allow a substantial price reduction and/or higher wages or prices for suppliers.

This can be illustrated by considering the case of residential care homes in the UK. The sector is capital intensive because the operator must always own or rent the building. Here target rates of return of 11–12% have been institutionalised in the calculations of the 'fair price of care' produced by the LaingBuisson consultancy every year since 2012; the 12% target reflects the business model of private equity care home chain owners and, relatedly, the prices paid for 60-bed homes which have in recent years been selling at around 8 times annual earnings.

In 2012, LaingBuisson calculated their fair price at 12% ROCE and in Exhibit 3.4 we have simply reworked their calculation counterfactually on the basis of an imputed 8% and 5% return for capital, with all other costs, including wages, held constant. At a 12% return the weekly total cost is £550, at 8% that drops to £493 and at 5% to £451; put simply, returning to the old world of 5% return on capital would reduce the cost of social care by 18% or nearly £100 per week. And the counterfactual is not entirely absurd because if care homes were publicly financed, 5% would be a sensible cost of capital right now (Burns *et al.* 2016).

Abstracted from this context, the LaingBuisson cost of care calculation is a powerful device. It has, for example, been accepted by English judges as a fair price calculation when operators go to court to ask for higher fee payments from local government authorities. But 12% is only a target and after more than five years of austerity cuts in local authority budgets, few, if any, English care home chains are reaching that target.

So the key question, not just for the care home sector but for numerous other privatised and outsourced foundational activities is: how can financial returns be levered up towards target? The answer is two-fold: first, by the use of power

Exhibit 3.4 UK residential care costs based on different return on capital assumptions[1]

Cost element of residential care	Cost per resident per week @ 12% ROCE (£)[2]	Cost per resident per week @ 8% ROCE (£)	Cost per resident per week @ 5% ROCE (£)
Staff costs	251	251	251
Repairs and maintenance	34	34	34
Other operating (non-staff) costs	95	95	95
Capital costs (imputed at different rates of return)	170	113	71
Cost per resident per week	**550**	**493**	**451**
Difference in cost per resident per week, compared with 12% return on capital assumption		–£57	–£99

Notes 1: The table is based on methodology by LaingBuisson. The data refers to provincial local authorities (excluding London) and is adjusted for inflation (2012 prices). 2: ROCE is the return on capital employed (the profit created in relation to total capital in the form of long term debt and/or equity). In the table, capital costs are calculated at three different rates of return on capital: 12% (which has been regarded as a 'fair' return by the industry), 8% and 5%.
Source: Burns *et al.* (2016, p. 32).

against stakeholders (labour, suppliers and consumers) to reduce costs or boost revenues; second, by using the devices of financial engineering not just to minimise tax liabilities but to strip operating subsidiaries of assets and burden them with liabilities. All this is illustrated below with UK cases: among the big economies of Europe, the UK has been a leader in privatisation and outsourcing which brings levered power and financial engineering into the foundational sectors; in the UK, there is also a tradition of radical accounting research using follow-the-money techniques. If we want to see a foundational future that does not work, the UK provides a cautionary tale.

Here are three levers and a couple of devices briefly described.

- Levering profits on labour is an effective strategy when labour-intensive foundational services operate in deregulated labour markets, allowing pay and conditions to be degraded. In the 2011–14 period, for example, prison officers in privatised UK prisons were earning less than £10 per hour, while their counterparts in public prisons were earning more than £14 (Bowman *et al.* 2015, p. 53). From leaked documents we know that the financial viability of private bids to take over public prisons depends entirely on the outsourcer's assumption that new hires will be paid lower wages.
- Where purchases account for a large percentage of sales, as in food retailing, then leverage can be applied against suppliers. This was the tactic in UK food retailing in the 1990s and 2000s, when four big supermarket chains were completely dominant, and processors were fearful of blacklisting. Exhibit 3.5 gives retailer, processor and farmer shares in the retail price of milk over fifteen years. Here the retailer applies power directly to the processor, whose share is squeezed so the retailers who took a few pence per litre off milk in the 1990s have been claiming 20 pence per litre since the mid-2000s (Bowman *et al.* 2014, pp. 69–70).

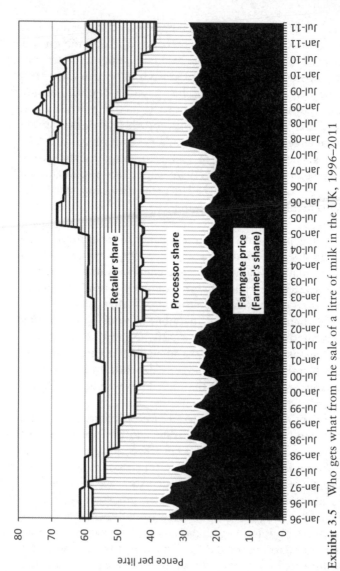

Exhibit 3.5 Who gets what from the sale of a litre of milk in the UK, 1996–2011
Note: The data is adjusted for inflation and presented in 2012 prices.
Source: DairyCo.

- Profits can be levered on consumers if there is scope for using confusion pricing to boost margins. A classic case is provided by the privatised UK energy supply sector. Confusion pricing here means special offers proliferate, and the number of tariffs multiplies so that it is extraordinarily difficult for the consumer to compare value for money and switch from one plan or provider to another. The predictable result is that captive customers are retained by the force of inertia. The British Gas utility's website in November 2017 listed 49 'old tariffs' and 23 more current offerings, with a bewildering variety of fixed prices, options on wholesale price movements, lock-in periods and exit fees, often available only to selected customers.[4]
- The simplest financial device for levering profit is cash extraction achieved via the balance sheet, classically by selling assets and/or burdening operations with debt or other liabilities like rent. Thus the Southern Cross care home chain was expanded to 750 homes by the Blackstone private equity house. Blackstone doubly profited because the private equity house floated the expanded chain as an operating company in 2006 and, separately, sold on the homes as a property company. There were two separate entities (operating company and property company) because the expansion of the chain had been funded by operating company sale and lease back of existing care homes with the property company. This was good for Blackstone's cash receipts but led to collapse of the chain within a few years because the property company was entitled to rent increases of 2.5% per annum, and the operating company collapsed in 2011 because it could not meet its rising rent bill.
- Another classic financial device is opportunist transactions, meeting short-term requirements for cash to hit quarterly earnings targets or boost the calculated internal rate of return. Thus special dividends can be extracted from subsidiaries or intra-group loans levied within complex

group structures which in both cases will transfer cash upwards to parents and leave asset-stripped and liability-burdened operating subsidiaries. For example, in 2013 Veolia's UK waste management subsidiary paid out a special dividend of £300 million to its French parent, financed by a group loan which increased the subsidiary's debt by more than £300 million; the parent gained from a dividend paid in cash and the subsidiary lost because it was left as an indebted firm with a new intra-group obligation to pay interest to its parent when it was operating in a difficult market (Bowman *et al.* 2015, pp. 82–91).

The levered use of power against stakeholders, coupled with the devices of financial engineering, destroyed the very social contract on which the corporate enterprise has rested, at least in the foundational economy. The old implicit social contract at corporate level rested on the idea of 'stream value' with benefits over time divided between stakeholders, where all had recognised claims on an ongoing operating business. Capital's claims were thus balanced against those of other stakeholders in long-term relations and with a shared interest in the operating business. After financialisation, through the application of levered power and financial engineering, we have the extraction of 'point value' which privileges returns to capital here and now, at this point in time in a specific enterprise. The beneficiary will be often not be an operating company but some kind of parent investor or holding company, whose commitment to individual operating subsidiaries depends on their contribution to meeting financial targets within short time horizons so that disposal and exit strategies are always in mind.

With point value, the aim is extraction of a return-at-one-node for immediate delivery as cash or capital gain for the equity or bond markets or fund investors. This is regardless of social consequences for stakeholders, economic consequences down the supply chain or the long-term requirements of a viable operating business. Various outcomes are possible: low wages pass the costs of wage subvention and old-age pensions to the state; suppliers without margins cannot afford to invest and slowly fail; confusion marketing feeds mis-selling to customers; and the devices of financial engineering increase the fragility of the operating subsidiaries of enterprises so that the long-term operating capability and robustness of operating subsidiaries are disregarded. These are the economic and social costs of extracting higher returns in foundational activities.

There are variations on the way financial engineering works, which depend in part on the investment requirements of the particular foundational sector. Consider the case of rail franchising under privatisation in the UK, where little or no investment is required. In the franchised operation of passenger trains, return on capital is irrelevant because operators such as Virgin Trains lease their trains and pay rental charges for access to the track infrastructure. Equally there is no product market risk because operators effectively have an option on profit: some operators have compensation clauses which cover slow growth of passenger numbers if GDP growth falters; all operators know that if, for any reason a franchise becomes unprofitable, the operator can walk away with little financial penalty.

Under the British system of regional rail franchising, the franchise operator claims to be an entrepreneur and can take out large amounts of profit. This is not justifiable under the rules of capitalism where profit is a reward for initial capital investment or subsequent exposure to revenue risk. These conditions are not met in rail franchising, though it is difficult to see this because there are quite complex flows of cash in and out of the operating company. Exhibit 3.6 lays out the complexities and Exhibit 3.7 summarises the net outcome in the case of Virgin on the West Coast line between London and the North. There was an initial modest investment of £20 million (quickly offset by selling a part stake to Stagecoach); over the next fifteen years this investment unlocked a state

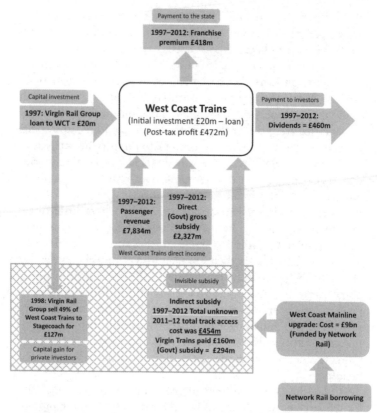

Exhibit 3.6 The UK West Coast Trains operating franchise: income, payments and extraction, 1997–2012
Source: Bowman *et al.* (2013b, p. 22).

subsidy of more than £2.5 billion. The figures completely dwarf franchise payments made by Virgin to the state and, as Exhibit 3.7 shows, nearly £500 million was then extracted as dividends by Virgin/Stagecoach. Returns of more than twenty times initial investment have attracted publicly owned mainland rail utilities as well as financialised British investors: Deutsche

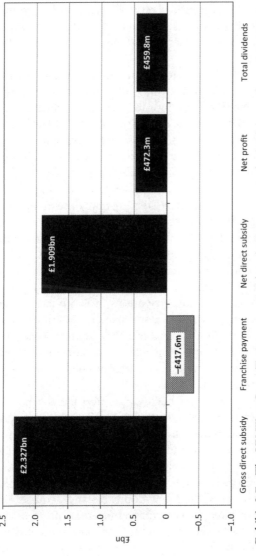

Exhibit 3.7 The UK West Coast Trains operating franchise: summary of subsidies, profits and dividends, 1997–2012

Source: Bowman *et al.* (2013a, p. 51).

Bahn, Keolis, Abellio and Trenitalia have stakes in half or more of the UK franchises, and these operators are wholly or partly owned by the German, French, Dutch and Italian Governments.

Much of what passes for franchising in the foundational economy looks like easy money in a kind of sham capitalist game where the franchisee bids for a contract which represents a low investment private option on profit where downside risk and responsibility for investment stays with the state. This no doubt explains the attractions of UK train franchising for mainland European state-owned utilities. But the game is often more complicated than this in outsourcing when the franchisee is a conglomerate under pressure for earnings growth and holding a diverse portfolio of contracts which do not all include provision for a low-cost walk-away from the obligation to provide service. These complications arise in the new world of financial engineering because stock market and fund investors want growth of earnings and capital value as well as high returns from outsourcing. Privatisation is a once-and-for-all process but, in the outsourcing business, contracts have to churn as existing, time-limited franchises expire. Growth only comes by replacing old contracts with more new ones and these new contracts are most easily obtained by moving into new areas of activity.

Thus the outsourcing business is increasingly dominated by conglomerates like Serco and G4S, who operate internationally in many activities, live by gaining contracts, grow by moving into new areas, and are prone to profits collapse when they bid for or acquire contracts which generate unexpected losses from unanticipated complications. In the case of Serco, a combination of adding new contracts and acquiring other firms with contracts increased revenues ten-fold to nearly £5 billion over the fifteen years after 1997 and built margins of around 4–6% on turnover from several hundred contracts. But profits collapsed as the company unexpectedly crashed into huge losses after taking on ill-judged contracts, like one to house UK asylum seekers which generated what the company itself described as 'shockingly large losses' (Bowman *et al.* 2015, p. 72). The fact that many individual outsourcing contracts are highly profitable does not prevent conglomerates with portfolios of contracts falling into crisis.

The alibi of those in the financial markets is that the stakeholder injuries and sector disorganisations described in this section serve a larger social good. It is all part of a virtuous process by which the financialisation of operations and assets produces cash streams that go to ordinary people through insurance and private pensions that depend on returns from the stock market, private equity and hedge funds. The problem is that the distribution of wealth is unequal, and citizens therefore have very unequal claims on the cash stream from financialised assets and operations held by funds. In the UK case, as we will show in Chapter 5, the top 30% of households hold around 80% of private pension wealth and other forms of (net) financial wealth. As in other European countries, half the citizens live in households with few assets of any kind so that the bottom 50% of UK households by income hold less than 10% of all wealth. There is therefore no credible (re) distributive social justification for the predations of financial engineering in the foundational economy.

The damage done

The UK illustrations show how, after privatisation and out-sourcing, the business models that shape the foundational economy were recast in a powerfully destructive direction. The UK is prototypical because it is a European leader in privatisation and outsourcing for maximum short-term gain from what historically were activities guided by long term horizons. But if the UK leads the way, there are plenty of cases in other European countries that illustrate the mechanics of exploitation and extraction. Here, to make that point, are two Italian cases. The case of Italian rail shows similar mechanisms in different contexts, while Italian care shows how there can be striking national differences in the way exploitation and extraction work.

First, consider the case of Italian railways. As we have seen, the British example is a textbook case of how to combine low risk with high returns, and to turn the result into a trade narrative of half-truths representing the result as a national success story. The story of Italian railways resembles the UK in this way: it is a story about passing responsibility for investment to the state, while positioning private operators for profitability. But the Italian story differs in two crucial respects: Italy has a two-speed railway system and passenger numbers are declining.

The context is provided by the EU's regulatory regime. Under EU liberalisation rules, Italy's state-owned rail company has been transformed into a holding company, Ferrovie dello Stato Italiane (FSI), which the Italian Government plans to privatise. FSI's Rete Ferroviaria Italiana subsidiary runs track and infrastructure, while its Trenitalia subsidiary operates train services. The government of Matteo Renzi (2014–16) was able to consider partial privatisation by selling shares in FSI because of a remarkable financial turnaround with the profit margin transformed from –10% in 2006 to 23% in 2013. As in the UK, private profit can be found in operating railways as long as the state takes responsibility for capital investment in infrastructure: the Program Contract for Investments financed investment projects worth about €94 billion in 2007–11, while for the period 2012–16 about €99 billion was allocated for infrastructure renewal and automation.

A critical difference between the two national cases is that profit in the Italian case was extracted while passenger kilometres travelled declined and the rail system was down-sized. Between 2006 and 2013, passenger kilometres declined by 20% and the fleet of rolling stock and the workforce were both nearly halved in size. Cutting the workforce faster than declining passenger numbers helps to explain the transformation in profitability but, just as important, is the shift from subsidised services with controlled fares towards market services. Between 2006 and 2014, FSI reduced operating costs by €1,077 million, raised earnings from subsidised service contracts (regional and state) by €552 million, and increased 'market' revenues by €652 million.

FSI has thus introduced a two-speed service. On the one hand it has created a market-led premium market service with modern fast trains, primarily creating links between big cities. Here, passenger revenue per kilometre is increasing. But public service railways are in decline, both in quantity and quality. State subsidies to FSI have increased, but in medium–long distance trains FSO is retreating as it operates old, slow trains which are losing market share to low-cost airlines like Ryanair. Many areas of Italy, especially inland, are losing their rail services: between 2006 and 2014, 1,187 km of rail network were closed and in 15 of 20 regions services were reduced between 2010 and 2014 (Legambiente 2014).

This comparison of rail in the UK and in Italy shows that with the same activity in a different national context, the processes of extraction can work in the same way; in both countries, when there is not enough money in the fare box, it is possible to make profits in train operating if the state covers investment without getting any reward either in the form of financial return or public service ethos.

The second case of reshaping foundational business models in social care is more interesting still. In both the UK and Italy, state funding cuts mean that care services are under revenue pressure, but the processes of extraction and exploitation work differently in Italy, where care services have been outsourced not to chain operators but to the third (voluntary) sector. As a result, there is no extraction for capital in Italy, but since the 2008 financial crisis there has been a growing problem of exploitation of labour as the third sector's revenue has been squeezed.

From the 1970s onwards, the retreating Italian state out-sourced care services to not-for-profit third sector organisations, which by 2011 employed almost two thirds of the total social care work force. After the 2008 crisis, the third sector came under pressure in care because its revenues were increasingly squeezed and uncertain as support was switched between different groups of beneficiaries, direct payments were made to beneficiaries, and there was a move away from the 'open public call' system of contracting out. Under these pressures, the 'not-for-profit' bodies that delivered social care took an exploitative turn and began to bear down on labour costs quite as ruthlessly as any private-sector profit driven operator.

Formally, exploitation was possible because national laws and regulations allowed low wages, precarious employment contractual conditions, and a move to job flexibility. The proportion of fixed-term workers and external contractors in the third sector doubled from 8% in 2001 to 16% in 2011, a level that was twice as high as in private firms. Informal exploitation through unpaid work was facilitated by the perceived social importance of the jobs and the idea that the third sector was still in some sense working on the 'fair side of the market'.

The Italian care sector therefore shows us a distinctive model of labour exploitation *without* value extraction for capital. The leverage is on labour, rather than service users or the public sector, both of which benefit from labour exploitation. The process is continuous yet of low intensity, therefore distinguishing it from point value for large profits after financialisation. The goal of exploitation is frequently organisational survival, rather than accumulation of capital. Third sector commitment to principles of non-profit and symbolic rewards are key instruments for exploitation and are often more effective than economic devices. The end result is the institutionalisation of a culture of exploitation which enjoys strong legitimacy and encounters weak opposition.

The mechanics are very different in Italian rail and social care, and the damage done is specific in each case, but the outcome is predictably the same as in the various British cases considered in the previous section. Across diverse sectors in different countries, exploitation and extraction set up processes of economic disorganisation whose general effect could be described as social disconnection. Since the 1980s, there has been a weakening of our capacity to impose the values of decency, reciprocity and restraint on the business world. The root of this weakness is financialisation, the process by which businesses are driven by the logics of maximising shareholding return and by financial engineering in the new world of finance for its own sake seeking high returns regardless of foundational activity characteristics.

In Karl Polanyi's famous account of capitalist development in the period of the UK industrial revolution, he described a process by which economic activity was disembedded (or disconnected) from its social context of norms and values in the surrounding society (Polanyi 1944). This process of disconnection is what is happening now to the foundational economy in the age of privatisation and outsourcing.

• First, there is a disconnection *from production*, as firms tend to abandon the path of productive capitalism where the gain comes from developing product or service markets. The operating business is necessary to reassure investors they are not investing in a Ponzi-type scheme. But, as shown in this chapter, operations will then be run for cash and the maximisation of income and capital gains through financial channels. The interests of shareholders and fund investors are now front and centre in business strategies, management calculation and firm organisation. This reframing has (at least) two serious implications for foundational infrastructure: it leads to capital rationing and, when the returns expectations are not satisfactory for the holders of capital, the result is 'capital strike' or industrial divestment. Hence the contrast between state-led and cross-subsidised national electrification programmes in the mid-twentieth century and the current slow roll-out of fast broadband by a multiplicity of investment-averse providers. The resulting contrast is striking. The mid-twentieth century national electricity grids were created by state investment. Fast broadband, the 'successor' to energy distribution in the foundational economy, is often not available outside major cities: a 2017 digital progress report in the EU found that 76% of homes in cities have access to fast broadband (of 30 mmpbs or better) but in rural areas only 40% of homes have access.[5]

Second, the cash extracting, capital gain maximising enterprise lives in a short-term world of quarterly earnings and 'enterprise value' – which is what the operating business is worth to the next acquirer. This tends to disconnect from the long term of social reproduction, foundational progress and technical change. The problems here go well beyond the officially recognised ones about the reluctance of financialised firms to invest in early stage innovation. As noted in this chapter, the fundamental problem is point value financial logic, which is rooted in appraisal techniques that bizarrely apply the discounting techniques originally developed for portfolio investment to productive decisions including those in the foundational economy (Bowman *et al.* 2014, pp. 124–6). At discount rates of 5% or more, distant earnings have little value and social benefits are ignored, so this calculus has a bias against foundational investment.

- A third form of disconnection affects the relationship between the firm and *the territory*, considered both as a physical locale and a networked, organisational space. From the point of view of financialised giant firms, suppliers and others must avoid damaging their corporate reputation, such as by employing child labour or producing unsafe products; but supply-chain leaders have no broad responsibility for providing the financial margins and continuous work flow that underwrites sustainability and responsibility down the chain. The archetypal model here is the relation between Apple and its assemblers, when Appple makes huge profits from designing, branding and selling smart phones that are assembled in China by marginally profitable Foxconn; or again, the publicly quoted supermarkets which will ask suppliers for price rebates if they are having a bad quarter. After financialisation, we have the replacement of exhausted suppliers and the rapid remodelling of supply chains, which are the characteristics of firms severing network ties in a social space and up-rooting from a territory and its immobile population.

- The fourth form of disconnection is disconnection *from work*. The rhetoric of human resources is important to present-day business and unintentionally declares its own limits, as it explicitly downgrades humans to means. Financialised firms tend to consider labour as a fixed cost to be reduced, as an obstacle between them and a higher return on capital. There are many ways to reduce labour costs. So-called 'labour law reforms' across Europe have liberalised the labour market: workforce reduction, flexible labour contracts, segmentation (and possibly relocation) of production processes, centralisation of coordination and control, reduction of margins of autonomy and of discretion in peripheral units. The organic two-way obligation between firm and worker is dissolved as workers may be considered as 'internal customers', not participating subjects.

From financial engineering to moral purpose

In its historical origins, the foundational economy was at heart a moral enterprise. That may seem elevated language, but how else to describe the great infrastructure projects designed to safeguard human health by supplying clean water and sanitation, or the great providential schemes that provided income support in sickness and old age and provided for the education of children? Opposing the wrecking of the foundational economy in the last generation is thus not just a matter of resisting predatory and unsuitable financial models. It is also about re-embedding the economy in social constraints and ambition. This project of re-moralising the economy already has the support of many. Here, for example, is Pope Francis in dialogue with redundant workers in a large Italian firm:

> A disease of the economy is the progressive transformation of entrepreneurs into speculators. The entrepreneur must not be confused with the speculator: there are two different types … We must fear the speculators, not the entrepreneurs … But paradoxically, sometimes the political system seems to encourage those who speculate on work and not those who invest in and believe in the job. (Vatican Press Service 2017)

But how do we rethink the sphere of the social and its connection with the politico-moral obligations of business? What is the nature of citizenship and its relation to territorial rights? These issues are considered in the next chapter.

Notes

1 For example, see the website of the International Consortium of Investigative Journalists: https://panamapapers.icij.org/ (accessed 8 February 2018) and https://www.icij.org/investigations/paradise-papers/ (accessed 8 February 2018).
2 At the point of privatisation, the benefits to the new owners included debt write-off of £5 billion and a 'green dowry' of £1.6 billion for the industry (Lobina and Hall 2001).
3 The rate of return on capital is calculated as the profits earned divided by the total amount of long-term capital employed in the

business. This capital consists of long-term debt (i.e. debt repayable beyond one year) and the equity or shareholders' funds. The ROCE is expressed as a percentage, i.e. the amount of profit earned per pound, euro or dollar of capital. Shareholder value is created if the return on the capital is more than the cost of the capital (which relates to the interest charges on the debt and the imputed cost of the equity).

4 See: https://www.britishgas.co.uk/energy/gas-and-electricity/tariffs-a-z.html (accessed 8 February 2018).
5 See: https://ec.europa.eu/digital-single-market/en/news/european-digital-progress-report-review-member-states-progress-towards-digital-priorities (accessed 8 February 2018).

4 The constitution of the foundational

The rights and duties of citizens

A man, e.g., has been allowed to drive at any pace he likes through the streets, to build houses without any reference to sanitary conditions, to keep his children at home or send them to work 'analphabetic', to buy or sell alcoholic drinks at his pleasure. If laws are passed interfering with any or all of these powers, he says that his rights are being violated. But he only possessed these powers as rights through membership of a society which secured them to him, and of which the only permanent bond consists in the reference to the well-being of its members as a whole. It has been the social recognition grounded on that reference that has rendered certain of his powers rights. If upon new conditions arising, or upon elements of social good being taken account of which had been over-looked before, or upon persons being taken into the reckoning as capable of participating in the social well-being who had previously been treated merely as means to its attainment, – if in any of these ways or otherwise the reference to social well-being suggests the necessity of some further regulation of the individual's liberty to do as he pleases, he can plead no right against this regulation. (T.H. Green, Lectures on the principles of *Political Obligation* (Green 1895/1941, pp. 147–8)

What does it mean to be a citizen and how should we deter-mine the duties of citizens and the rights that citizens have to foundational goods and services? In this chapter our argument turns to issues of moral economy, political philosophy and the principled basis of state action in the foundational sphere. These issues may seem abstract to twenty-first-century readers but were seen as unavoidable in the first municipal age of the foundational after 1880, because the new entitlements to education and clean water came with a whole series of obligations, such as to send children to school, to construct houses according to building regulations and such like. All this restricted the established freedom of individuals as parents, householders or publicans to do as they pleased. Hence, the opening quotation comes from the English radical liberal philosopher and Oxford municipal reformer, T.H. Green. He argued, at the close of the nineteenth century, that the touchstone was always the social well-being of all members of society and, as ideas of well-being had changed with the foundational revolution, so individual citizen rights and duties would inevitably change and the sphere of state action (especially at municipal or local state level) would increase.

Up to the late 1940s, this kind of explicit, liberal collectivist philosophy was central to Keynes and Beveridge's thinking when they envisaged limited state intervention and a new role for intermediate, non-state institutions to secure employment levels and welfare within a capitalist host economy (see Cutler, Williams and Williams, 1986.) It was also significant in subsequent mainland European thinking by figures like Alfred Müller-Armack and Ludwig Erhard about a social market economy which would combine social welfare provision and the enforcement of competition to prevent the economic abuse of corporate power. But, by the 1960s, we had Keynesianism without Keynes, so that demand management through fiscal means could be discussed as a technical policy for 'steering the economy' without recognising the broader context of Keynes' thinking, especially in *The End of Laissez Faire* (1926), about the role of intermediary institutions which are outside of the state and the market but play important roles in promoting social objectives.

The aim of this chapter is to re-establish the connection between technical policy and political philosophy which has (despite spirited challenges) since been ossified by the tripartite academic division of labour between economics, politics and sociology. Against this we would echo Boltanski and Thévenot's (2006) argument that in modern society there are multiple orders of worth and principles of evaluation: in other words, we should avoid simple, one-dimensional measures of value. The foundational economy is then the domain which spans technics, history, economy and moral philosophy in an untidy relation of contest so that issues of moral economy and political philosophy are inseparably part of foundational thinking.

When that has been said, many will be puzzled by a chapter titled 'The constitution of the foundational'. The Oxford English Dictionary defines a constitution as 'a body of fundamental principles or established precedents according to which a state or other body is acknowledged to be governed'. This is the constitution thought of as a political mechanism – a set of rules prescribing the relationship between the different parts of a state, institutional and territorial, and the processes of representative democracy like parliamentary terms and the powers of the head of state. Historically, constitutions have tended to be silent on substantive, rather than procedural, issues. And even when not silent – as in the case of the Italian Constitution created after the Second World War – the practice of constitutional argument virtually ignores substantive economic issues.

But there is another tradition in thinking about constitutions. It starts not with governmental institutions but with the key component of the polity – the citizen. What does it mean to be a citizen? The most influential European answer to that question was provided by T.H. Marshall in his 1950 essay on social citizenship. Here history is represented as 'the enrichment of the status of citizenship through the progressive extension of rights from eighteenth-century civil rights through nineteent-century political rights to twentieth-century social welfare' (Marshall 1950, p. 33). Marshall's answer was, of course, partial – implicitly he provided an account of the gains made by male, working-class citizens in high-income countries in the 100 years up to the 1950s. We all now accept that there is more to entitlement than this.

But the substantive constitutional question about citizen rights and duties is important because it forces us to think about a set of fundamental issues that go to the heart of what a functioning foundational economy is and does. In this chapter, our answer to the substantive question comes in three parts, which combine to offer a view of what the constitution of the foundational economy is and should be. Our argument is about the rights of individuals as natural persons and the duties of corporations as juridical persons. And from the orders of worth point of view, the argument is important because it adds a normative element which shows that the foundational economy is more than a descriptive economic observation or a classificatory device.

The history of the foundational sketched in Chapter 2 shows that it emerged as an answer to an implicit question about what constitutes fundamental human needs. (Answer, in part: things like clean water.) And in the first section of this chapter we pose and answer this question about needs explicitly by considering argument and evidence about how foundational provision is immanently, that is to say implicitly, moral as it works to define citizenship through entitlement. To that extent, present-day foundational practice is grounded in (unacknowledged) moral economy and political philosophy.

In the second section of the chapter we consider how this coupling of foundational economy and citizen entitlement creates problems because such entitlements vary territorially even within high-income Western Europe. We can no longer assume, as did T.H. Marshall, that a natural process of historical evolution would bring citizens ever more entitlements.

Our response is that the foundational core is not a list of citizen entitlements specific to a territory, but arises from a set of political-moral choices which cannot be derived from the decisions made by governing systems for the one place at a specific moment of time. There is an irreducible core to foundational provision that is detachable from local territorial choices.

The question of territorial choice recurs in the third section which turns to one of the major constitutional issues of our time. We know from Chapter 3 that the recent history of the foundational economy is partly about predation following privatisation and outsourcing. Citizens may have voted for the market and efficiency; what they got was high-return business models plus disorganisation and disembedding of the foundational economy through the devices of extraction and exploitation. That has created a huge problem that is in essence constitutional: how can the new corporate powerholders be controlled?

Section three turns to this problem of corporate power without foundational responsibility. The starting point is straightforward and a commonplace of company law: corporations are juridical persons with many of the same rights as natural persons. This third section argues that the duties of corporate actors operating in a foundational sphere should be made explicit and the private companies active in these areas should be brought within a reframed constitution.

The moral basis of foundational provision

It has long been recognised that economies do have moral foundations and that the behaviour of economic institutions and individuals should be guided by moral ends. In the classical economic literature, Adam Smith's *Wealth of Nations* (1776) is underpinned by his *Theory of Moral Sentiments* (1759) which invokes 'pity or compassion, the emotion we feel for the misery of others, when we either see it, or are made to conceive it' and insists that the happiness of others is necessary though we derive no material benefit from it.

All this is lost sight of after the late nineteenth century insofar as mainstream economics increasingly is an edifice built on the work of W.S. Jevons and Alfred Marshall, and relies on marginal utility to explain the behaviour of atomised consumers. More recently, Kahneman and Tversky (1979) have elegantly undermined marginalism by demonstrating experimentally that the choices of human subjects are inconsistent and judgements depend on the framing of choice. But mainstream economics remains epistemologically hostile to the normative because many economists maintain a positivist distinction between fact and value in the hope of demarcating a scientific and value-free economics (Earle, Moran and Ward-Perkins 2017, pp. 93–9). As Sayer (2011) points out, social scientists are also guilty of misframing fact-value dualisms.

And yet the normative never goes away if, as Sayer (2000, p. 79) argues, 'the moral economy embodies norms and sentiment regarding the responsibilities and rights of individuals and institutions with respect to others'. Every capitalist society generates norms and regulations relating to how much inequality is acceptable, what can and cannot be commodified, who should work, what is acceptable pay and conditions of work and who (e.g. minors) should be protected. Such minimum socially defined standards coexist as governing principles – and therefore moral choices – alongside any consumer choice exercised by individuals within a market.

But direct inference of citizen rights from publicly declared principles encounters the problem that high principles are not always honoured. Few will argue openly for immorality as an organising principle in social life, but public life often rests on the principle of breaching political regulations and avowed moral principles. For example: Italy and the UK maintain textiles sectors in Prato (Froud *et al.* 2017) and Leicester (Hammer 2015, pp. 31–40), where many employers breach national rules on wages and conditions. Against this background, how can the foundational economy claim a moral grounding?

The answer lies in understanding the intersection of two things: the historical processes by which the foundational economy was built, and the analytical investigations by which philosophers have sought to arrive at a picture of identifiable human capabilities. We can take the latter first, since it is an initial step in the exercise of seeing what a moral (foundational) economy is and ought to be.

In the work of Sen, the philosopher best known for this analysis, human capabilities are linked to the idea of the good life and the possibilities for human flourishing (Sen 1999). The capabilities approach sets out a path for assessing social, political and economic systems against their effect on human flourishing and well-being. Moreover, Nussbaum (2000) has extended this to a rights-based approach, which constructs lists of capabilities that should be enshrined in constitutions (accepting that capabilities can vary cross-culturally). These arguments can be linked to citizenship, as Lockwood's work shows, because 'civic expansion' through new rights enables individuals to participate and flourish (Lockwood 1996).

The important point is that, for Sen and Nussbaum, economic resources are not a technical input to production but a politico-moral means to well-being and flourishing; individual internal capacities and skills interact with external structural factors to determine capabilities. This does ground foundational provision philosophically and morally but in a very analytic and abstract way. If we turn now to examine the historical development of the foundational economy we can see a kind of practical working out of the theory of human needs and human capabilities, because foundational provision amounts to a kind of immanent (implicit) moral theory of citizenship.

At origin, admittedly, foundational provision hardly amounted to an implicit theory of human capabilities, and 'gas and water socialism' of the kind described in Chapter 2 had much more limited purposes. Water – or rather clean, healthy water – was the original foundational good. At its most generous, the drive for clean water, expressed in the construction of reservoirs and sanitary sewage systems, was based on a minimalist moral purpose – avoiding mass deaths caused by the spread of diseases like cholera. At its most defensive it can be understood as a reaction by the propertied and prosperous to the health risks posed by infectious diseases among the poor; though it also reflected a degree of enlightened capitalist self-interest as collective solutions that, for example, provided networks of clean water and energy which were also beneficial to industrial development. But over time a more comprehensive and expansive moral vision inhered in the development of foundational services, even in the material domain.

From this point of view, the rise of Gordon's networked household in the US was a landmark achievement because it plugged the individual household into a range of material foundational networks – water and energy in particular – and then coupled this with innovative domestic technologies around new durables like vacuum cleaners, cookers and refrigerators (Gordon 2016). Thus networks transformed not only productivity but also the conditions of everyday life, notably the working conditions of women in the home. In short, this was a practical revolution in human capabilities, a realisation of how women, especially, could be lifted out of domestic drudgery.

Some of the entrepreneurs central to these innovations had an inkling of the social consequences of what they were doing. Thus Henry Ford did have a social vision (albeit a gendered one), suitably commemorated in the term 'Fordism', which describes an economy of high wages and mass durable consumption. But most of the firms, like Hoover and GEC, which met the new demands, were just making money from mass-producing consumer durables, not developing a social vision of domestic liberation. It is therefore important to shift the focus from the durable machine to the systems that underlay the creation of much of the material foundational economy, and thus of the networked household.

The reach, availability and pricing of foundational system access contains powerful implications for entitlement and therefore for what can reasonably be called citizenship. Three such implications are particularly important:

- First, relatively few of the goods and services of the foundational economy were free public goods; many involved some charge at the point of consumption. But many, from water to public transport, were subsidised on a scale designed to ensure that everyone in the community – not just adult citizens or families in the top quintile of incomes – had access to them as a basic condition of being able to function and develop as human beings. This calculus also explains why health and school education were generally free-at-point-of-use because these services are seen as critical to human development and capability, given our prevailing concepts of the common good and social welfare.

- Second, many of the key goods and services created by the material foundational economy, though territorially bounded, are universal in reach within a bounded territory. An alternative way of putting this is that they are contiguous with geographically bounded territorial units, notably the nation state – as most obviously with the creation of pipeline grid networks or electrification projects within state boundaries. An obvious consequence of this is that they are shaped not only by general conceptions of human need but by changing notions of citizenship entitlement, and by variations in those conceptions between different political jurisdictions.

- Third, the moral dimension of the material domain is not just a matter of its physical provision, but of its regulation and ownership. The most obvious example of the latter over time is the way environmental regulation of emissions is shaped by the aim of safeguarding clean air and clean water. A further example is provided by the regulation of the structures which deliver the goods and services of the material domain: their ownership structures, pricing policies and so forth. The conclusion to that is obvious: the conceptions of the conditions needed for the realisation of human capabilities are not fixed, but constantly have to be negotiated, partly by a process of political struggle and partly by a process of scientific inquiry. A classic example is provided by the British Clean Air Act of 1956: in what was then a coal-burning country, the Act sought (successfully) to reverse the visible pollution that had such catastrophic health consequences. A contemporary example is provided by the way that many of Europe's largest cities are now beginning to engage with invisible particulate pollution from diesel exhaust and other sources, which causes thousands of premature deaths each year in every major city.

Thus our argument is that the foundational economy has, from the beginning, performed a moral economy: that is, the goods and services it provides enact some conception of the good life, even though it is rare for that conception to be expressed in such elevated terms. Foundational provision and entitlement is the practical analogue of the large theoretical literature on human needs and human capabilities. It provides a material and specific context in which we should understand Sen and Nussbaum's abstract and general arguments about capability. To that extent, the foundational economy is morally and philosophically grounded.

If foundational provision is inherently normative, it is neither the product of abstract philosophical reasoning nor of a once-and-for-all vision of what is needed for the realisation of human capabilities. It is a historically created moral economy, specific to a time and place, the product of a complex mix of political struggle, technical innovation and scientific investigation. And citizen entitlement will vary according to time and place because, prima facie, that entitlement is connected to territories and to the changing shape and capacities of units of government at supra-national, state and sub-state levels. In other words, the foundational economy is not only a moral economy – it is also a political economy, and it is to this that we turn in the next two sections of this chapter about citizen rights and duties.

The next section takes up the most obvious question arising. Our argument is that the moral foundations of the foundational economy are revealed by what it actually does. But, as we have just observed, what the foundational economy actually does varies by territory and time. If that is so, can the foundational economy have some kind of core which can be detached from territory?

The foundational economy and its spatial limits

The idea of citizenship and the idea of the foundational economy share this one important feature: they are simultaneously both general in character and spatially bounded. At the core of the foundational economy, as the previous section made clear, is a general conception of what should constitute human capabilities – or, as we have re-defined it, a changing social conception at different historical moments of how those capabilities should be realised through citizen rights. Yet at the same time, the foundational economy has usually had a spatially bounded reality: in some instances of the material domain, it is exactly spatially delineated by the character of physical distribution networks for water, waste disposal and energy; in the case of the providential domain it is most closely identified with the creation within nations of what we conventionally call the welfare state.

The idea of citizenship exhibits a similar duality. As is well known, the root of the word is in a territorial identity – the city. And in the modern world, by far the most successful citizenship projects have been territorially delimited, associated with the historical project of the nation state. Citizenship thus simultaneously includes and excludes. You do not have to be a post-colonial theorist to see that the processes which confer political voice and welfare entitlements on a high-income, urban and industrial population inside a West European state will always exclude, and may actively subordinate, external populations which can then be represented as some alien 'other' in crude and reductive ways (Morris 2016).

The exclusionary character of citizenship is such that access to the providential domain ordinarily depends on having the political status of a citizen of that territory. Citizenship can be acquired in various ways (including by purchase in an EU country like Malta) but is semi-automatically granted by right of birth within the territory or by parental attachment to the territory: in other words, by links of blood or soil. Against this background, access can also be a contingent concession which a national territory makes, such as allowing residents who are citizens of other EU countries to access its providential domain. At the same time, the EU 28 have an agency, Frontex (the European Border and Coast Guards Agency) dedicated to the work of policing their external borders against the incursion of migrants who would claim access to foundational goods as much as to waged employment.

The analytical point here is that the rights of citizenship are relative and territorially grounded. They cannot be claimed against some absolute standard but only against the standards of citizenship relative to the territorial domain where they are to be exercised. At the beginning of liberal collectivist thinking, this point was very clearly and explicitly made by T.H. Green, who was quoted at the beginning of this chapter. Green wrote in his *Principles of Political Obligation* that 'A right against society, in distinction from a right to be treated as a member of society, is a contradiction in terms' (Green 1895/1941, p. 110).

This analytical point is of great practical importance because, even within the providential domain in the EU, entitlements are not standardised. Benefits may be received on the basis of foreign social insurance contributions within the EU. But there is substantial national variation in the range of services, benefit entitlements and delivery systems available to citizens in various countries. What common level of provision and service delivery, if any, exist in the face of demonstrable national variations; and what principles of universal access, if any, can be invoked in a world where citizen entitlements are subject to territorial boundaries?

These boundaries are often narrower than the nation state because internal redistribution within one nation state often does not equalise financial resources and providential provision. This is a particular issue in Italy, where regional redistribution is contested and, for example, healthcare is much more gener- ously funded in the north than in the south of the country. A 2014 study found that, after correcting for demographic differences, health expenditure per person was 48% lower in Campania than in the Aosta Valley in the north (Cichetti and Gasbarrini 2016, p. 2).

Against this background, an obvious question arises: is there any fixed core to the foundational economy which can exist independently of territorial variations? There are basically two ways of answering this question. The first answer is in the spirit of T.H. Marshall's account of citizenship and social class, and implies an evolutionary history where the character of entitlements is revealed by the passage of time. The second (and in our view more credible) answer thickens the notion of citizenship by detaching it from territory and attaching it to moral choices.

The practical workings of the foundational economy do indeed suggest a core set of entitlements, starting historically with the most basic, such as the entitlement to water supplies, which do not constitute a danger to public health, and expand- ing over time with advances in technology (the creation of the networked household) and the expansion of the providential domain (the welfare state). But arguments for a defensible core of entitlements, derived from its observed evolution, simply reproduce all the problems of Marshall's evolutionary history.

If the character of entitlements is revealed by the passage of time, that revelation is highly variable by territory. Esping Andersen (1990) distinguished between liberal, conservative and social democratic types of welfare, broadly typified by the US, German and Swedish systems. And we now know that many national systems messily combine features of different types: so, is the irreducible core of entitlement to be American parsimony or Swedish generosity? And how do we deal with the experience of the last generation in the UK where the process of civic gain went into reverse to create an age of austerity and ongoing cuts in entitlement, while privatisation and outsourcing produced the new disorganisation, as outlined in Chapter 3?

If assumptions about evolution and revelation do not disclose an irreducible core, this suggests that a more ambitious strategy is required. A second solution therefore to the problem lies in 'thickening' the meaning of citizenship by disconnecting it from its historical links with territory, and transforming its meaning into something that is part of the very essence of being human and social. In taking this path, we are building on the strategy of the human capabilities approach discussed earlier. In the hands of a philosopher like Nussbaum the strategy not only disconnects entitlement from particular territorial settings, but also emphasises the way policy choices necessarily have to be moral choices.

It also ensures a second kind of disconnection, in opening up the possibility of disconnecting the choices in building the foundational economy from some predetermined list. Since the choices to be made are moral choices, they are also necessarily, in any particular context, contestable. We do not need a 'list' of the ideal citizen entitlements that should be 'supplied' by the foundational economy, but we do need a way of conceiving of citizenship which detaches it from territory and attaches it to moral choices.

One way of doing this is suggested by Weale's attempt to define citizenship beyond borders (Weale 1991). He begins by distinguishing between 'the identity aspect' and 'the normative aspect' of citizenship (Weale 1991, p. 157.) The normative (moral) face of citizenship means that entitlements and duties do not have to be restricted to a particular territorial group at any particular moment. There are both analytical and practical policy reasons for this.

Analytically, the identity of those who have entitlements and duties cannot be restricted to a set of humans at any particular historical moment, for to do so would be to deny the claims of future generations. Practically, many important policy problems – environmental protection, migration, capital flows, regulation of transnational enterprise – also involve cross-national interdependencies or temporal consequences, and therefore cannot defensibly only be conceived in a world of state delimited territorial boundaries in the here and now. In the foundational economy, for example, when a national health or social care system is staffed with foreign labour, that process has consequences for the national systems from which migrant labour is attracted – and, as in this example, potentially damaging consequences.

The result is that ideas of citizenship rights and entitlement – which undoubtedly lie at the heart of the foundational economy – cannot just be derived from the choices made by and for the citizens inside particular governing territorial systems at particular moments. These here and now decisions necessarily have consequences for those who are unheard and unfranchised – either because they have not yet been born or because they are excluded from the jurisdiction. Contestable and difficult though it is, the meaning of the entitlements which the foundational economy should deliver have to be morally informed.

The implication is that the foundational economy is what we as individual citizens of a territory have to take politico-moral responsibility for, while respecting those who do not have voice or franchise. Entitlement can be – and should be – detached from the territory which grants rights to the current population. As T.H. Green envisaged in the quotation that opened this chapter, the calculus of social well-being would change with 'persons being taken into the reckoning as capable of participating in the social well-being who have previously been treated as means to its attainment'.

Green was, then, advocating the extension of the franchise to property-less working men in a country where, after the 1884 Reform Act, all women and nearly half of adult men did not have the vote. But the principle is much wider, often applicable to everyday political choices and could be trans-formational if it were seriously operationalised. In 2015, the Welsh Government passed the Well Being of Future Generations (Wales) Act which requires existing public bodies and new Public Service Boards to think about the long-term impact of their decisions on sustainable development and seven well-being goals.[1]

But that is, as yet, an aspirational ideal and in the EU response to migrants who cross the Mediterranean by boat (as on many other issues) we see the abject failure of the political classes and their citizenry to meet the T.H. Green standard and to recognise Syrian or sub-Saharan migrants as 'persons capable of participating in the social well-being'. So we must consider the practical reality that citizens will vote, maybe confusedly or narrowly, to restrict entitlement directly, or vote for policies like tax cuts which have implications for entitlement.

There is a further major complication. In all the discussion so far of citizen rights, citizens have been discussed as though they were natural persons with gender, occupational histories, families and social lives. But companies and investors can, through incorporation, become juridical persons. In many jurisdictions, including the UK and the US, corporations are legal persons with the capacity to employ, sue, enter contracts, acquire property and incur debt. And they can do all this as corporate entities separate from their individual members who, under the rules of limited liability, are not responsible for their debts.

At the heart of the foundational economy is a kind of dualism, as this is increasingly a space where individual citizens face corporate citizens. On the demand side there are individuals making claims for services like clean water and energy, and income support in the providential domain; on the supply side, after the wrecking of the foundational, including through privatisation and outsourcing, there are companies responsible for delivering goods and services. If these companies are legal persons with large powers and privileges, they are effectively corporate citizens and it is reasonable to inquire about their rights and duties. This is especially the case when, as Chapter 3 made plain, we find inappropriate behaviours of corporates in the foundational domain.

The next section of this chapter therefore considers the complications created by corporate power in the foundational economy.

Corporate citizens in the foundational economy

It is all very well to argue abstractly, as we have, that the foundational economy in a democracy should be about more than the choices of franchised citizens in a specific territory at one moment in time. But, in thinking about foundational provision in present-day European democracies, we must recognise practically the decisions of franchised citizens who will not always or usually vote to extend entitlements within their territory in a progressive way. T.H. Marshall in 1950 could assume an extension of entitlements and Esping Andersen in 1990 could classify the variation in entitlement, but approaching 2020 we must answer a darker question. What is the principled objection to democratic choice when the governing body of any jurisdiction has an electoral mandate from the citizens to reorganise the foundational economy on neoliberal principles (and incidentally restrict entitlement)?

From the British examples described in Chapter 3, we know that this ends in disillusion. The citizenry is promised the market and efficiency but, through privatisation and outsourcing, the result is something very different: a huge aggrandisement of corporate power and disorganisation of the foundational, working through the devices of extraction and exploitation and the import of unsuitable business models from high-risk, high-return activities. By 2017, more than three-quarters of British respondents in opinion polls believed that four key utilities (rail, water, gas and electricity) should be in the public sector, and support for renationalisation is remarkably constant across all age groups (Elliott and Kanagasooriam 2017, pp. 14–15).

The UK has these privatised utilities because, in the 1979–2010 period, Thatcher and Blair each won three successive elections. And if naïve electoral enthusiasm for enterprise has waned since the financial crisis of 2008, confusions continue. Rich European regions like Catalonia and Lombardy Veneto contain secessionists who mix cultural identity politics with demands for regional autonomy and fiscal federalism. The scapegoating of dependent regions may then be downplayed by parties like Lega Nord when they seek national power; but the logic of their position is restriction of national redistribution to poorer regions. Across Europe, centre-right and populist politicians enthuse about lower taxes, while cultivating their voting bases with narrow and misleading welfare promises focused on pensions and healthcare.

An intellectual critique of these observed confusions is not the same as an effective political response, which requires some prior analysis of what has gone wrong and how it can be put right. And here the concepts of citizenship rights and duties can again provide a starting point. If we look beyond the economic mess of extraction, exploitation and disorganisation, we see that privatisation and outsourcing created a political anomaly. These processes hugely empowered fund investors and corporate actors, who as juridical persons gained rights without duties. As Chapter 3 argued, economics-based regulation of specific utility services was completely ineffectual, and now we would add the point that the rhetoric of competitivity more generally undermined any possibility of insisting on the duties of corporations.

Under EU competition policy, sectoral aids by national governments are discouraged, as they undermine a level playing field. National industrial policy and regional policy was, then, transformed into a kind of beauty contest to produce a more competitive environment which would attract and retain mobile business, on the assumption that the territory with the more burdensome environment would lose the contest. The 'business friendly' result was an attempt to manage (all) private business by carrots, without sticks. Policy was a matter of incentives to corporate enterprise in the form of tax cuts, debt relief privileges and state-funded gifts, including infrastructure improvement and skills training. Lest business felt unloved, tax avoidance through blatantly artificial schemes was widely condoned.

These policies flew in the face of historical experience: successful industrial policy in Japan and Korea had offered rewards conditional upon firms delivering performance, and industries accepting restructuring.[2] In contrast, European policies for competitivity were expensively unfocused because the central state gave concessions (like lower corporation tax rates) to all businesses, which mostly did what they were going to do in any case. Foundational activities employing 40% of the workforce in each national economy should have been exempted from the regime of give-aways because their activities were mainly immobile when anchored by distribution networks to specific populations. But the foundational was invisible, and economic policy in Europe treated private business as though it was all mobile and footloose and needed to be offered privileges and concessions lest it shift operations to other, more attractive sites.

Within this competitivity frame, policymakers competed to offer privileges, losing sight of the old liberal collectivist presumption that, if the state offered big business privileges (like joint stock organisation or state funded infrastructure), then corporations should in return accept obligations. The American liberal collectivist Adolf Berle (1962) had written of a 'tacit social contract' between the corporation and society, but that seems to have vanished after 1980. Consider, for example, grocery retailing. In most West European countries, a handful of supermarket chains like Carrefour and Tesco built dominant positions on the basis of planning permissions which give their large, edge-of-town branches first claim on the grocery spend of households in a locality; nothing was ever required in return as social quid pro quo.

After privatisation and outsourcing, newly powerful corporate actors were doubly released from social obligation by the sector-specific ineffectuality of economics-based regulation and by the more general collapse of earlier liberal collectivist ideas about how corporate rights should be balanced by duties. The corporates in the foundational economy functioned as juridical citizens without any specification of their duties. Privatisation and outsourcing had created mighty corporations as private actors who were largely exempt from the obligations that we expect to impose on public bodies.

Our inference is plain but radical. One proper response to the political and economic mess described above is to insist that private corporate actors and investment vehicles operating in the material and providential domains should be brought within the constitution. To be clear, constitutions are not simply about specifying how representative democracy works through a formal political apparatus. Implicitly or explicitly, by silence or voice, constitutions also answer two key questions: what should be the boundaries of public jurisdiction, and, once those boundaries are established, what should be the rules that govern the behaviour of institutions which are in the public sphere?

The constitution of the foundational economy since the era of predation began has been a constitution of silences on these key questions: powerful corporate actors have been given access to public services and public money, but without any corresponding obligations beyond service delivery. The giant outsourcing companies like G4S and Sodexo have, in a shadowy way, become governing institutions with much power and little responsibility. The answer is to make their obligations explicit and morally defensible, not by renationalisation, which changes ownership, but by constitutional reform which brings them into the public domain and subjects them to a new kind of regulation.[3]

This approach is novel because ownership is now used everywhere as the decision principle for identifying what is private or public (with member-owned not-for-profit organisations in an intermediate position). Privatisation and outsourcing generally puts foundational service delivery into the hands of privately owned operators, so that train operators or care home chains are, in many ways, then officially regarded as outside the public domain in the same way that privately owned supermarket chains or retail banks have always been. In foundational thinking, the alternative decision principle is *function*. If firms are providing welfare-critical foundational services, like retail banking or adult care, they should be treated as *in* the public domain regardless of ownership. And that applies to newly privatised utilities, recently grown giant outsourcing conglomerates and long-established private providers like supermarket chains (as well as to mutuals because, as we saw in Chapter 3, absence of the profit motive is no guarantee of social virtue).

The assumption that private providers are outside the public domain has major consequences for status and governance. UK company law uniquely treats the corporation as a private association and has been reluctant to intervene in its internal affairs. Right across Europe, the internal governance of the new foundational providers is (as with old providers), the subject of corporate law, not public law. There are differences between jurisdictions about what kind of organisations can claim legal personality, but everywhere in Europe the corporation is treated as a juridical person with domicile, which can enter into contracts, sue, employ individuals, acquire assets and incur debt; the privilege of company registration with limited liability is cheaply available through off-the-shelf incorporation.

This may have been acceptable in an earlier period, when the state had a working model for its procurement relations with a private contractor supplying non-foundational goods and services, like army boots or civil service filing cabinets. The established organisation of public procurement enforced arms-length relations by relatively straightforward rules about, for instance, costs, confidentiality and the impartiality of rules governing the selection of contractors through due process. But the modern privatised utility or outsourcing giant delivers complex packages of public goods and services which cannot be managed through the practice of sealed bids for contracts delivered on a spot date.

As we have argued, new kinds of economics-based sector-specific regulation did not address business models, and the parallel insistence on 'business friendly' concessions more generally undermined any possibility of controlling corporate behaviours. As centrist politicians literally did not know what else to do, privatisation and outsourcing quickly became games that the state had to keep going. Many public utilities were networked in ways which created natural monopolies; the most important forms of outsourcing offered long-term operating franchises without which corporate bidders would simply not appear in the market. So, competition for the market when franchises were re-let had to substitute for competition in the market, as in the case of UK rail franchising. Or, competition in the market had to take the form of different supplier tariffs from the same infrastructure, as in EU telecoms where smaller competitors are supposed to be able to access the networks of large operators.

Competition in the market and for the market have both produced disappointing outcomes because neither providers nor consumers in the privatised utilities were interested in behaving in the ways that were necessary if competition and markets were to deliver efficiency and lower prices. If the state wants the outsourcing game to continue, franchises must be let on attractive terms to induce bids. Thus, in UK train franchising, the franchise has to offer an option to walk away with modest financial penalties if profits do not materialise; otherwise, firms like Virgin and Stagecoach will not bid. Where price competition in the market has materialised, however, passive consumers were exploited by energy suppliers relying on consumer inertia; while they also made retail price comparisons more difficult through confusion pricing. The consumer-driven model has been premised on the bizarre idea that citizens are not busy with all the everyday demands of work and family life, but are instead 'rational', one-dimensional calculating machines with a passion for price comparison websites.

As for direct control through outsourcing contracts, insofar as they could be written at all in terms of costs and key performance indicators, they were almost classics of incompleteness. In those circumstances, only high relations of trust, and complete commitment to public purpose, could bridge the gap. Even to say this is to see at once that this was a ludicrously optimistic hope. The privatised utilities or outsourcing giants are driven by forces far from a public purpose character. Fund investors in private companies, or public companies under stock market pressure will have no inhibitions about using the devices of extraction and exploitation, as detailed in

Chapter 3, to deliver on rate of return targets. Financialised conglomerates will also pursue growth regardless of the risk inherent in a diverse and complex portfolio of contracts.

But the fault here is not primarily with the outsourcing companies themselves, and still less with managers who happen to find themselves responsible for them. It lies with the constitutional order prevailing after the recent revolution in the organisation of the foundational economy. In essence, an implicit and disorganised constitutional system has developed, in which the privatised utilities and outsourcing giants are treated as private actors like contractors, even though they hold a public monopoly. They have been given public privileges – not to mention public money – without any recognition of how this involves the acceptance of public duties. It is, therefore, vital that this public service industry be subjected to an explicit framework which can be the basis for a new constitutional settlement.

How would this new constitutional order be different? The first and most obvious change would be that, since the institutions of the foundational economy are delivering basic public services, they must have public status. Those engaged in the foundational economy, whether private contractors or not-for-profit operators under various social and co-operative ownership arrangements, should be given the status of public bodies and not simply treated as private associations. A second implication follows from this: that the institutions delivering services in the foundational economy, since they are public bodies, should be subjected to the same general ethical standards as public bodies. Beyond this, relevant and activity-specific service requirements should be set for individual major providers under a system of social licence.

In the UK, the Committee on Standards in Public Life has already made some progress with specifying general ethical standards and applying them to outsourcing. Early on in its history, the Committee elaborated a set of 'principles of public life', including accountability, openness and honesty. These have clear implications for standards of conduct, for instance in the transparency governing the declaration of interests by public officials or the rules governing public appointments. They have equally clear implications for the organisation of privatised utilities and outsourced services, where we should not tolerate multi-tier corporate structures and complex intra-group transactions which create opacity and tax avoidance opportunities.

The Committee's report about outsourcing and its follow-up guidelines for providers mark an important breach with the past, and anticipate our argument that outsourcing companies be subject to the same ethical standards as public bodies (Committee on Standards in Public Life 2014; 2015.) Some of their recommendations do bear on business practices: for instance, a code for supply chains, and for the payment of the living wage. But in the main their recommendations bear on procedure not substance: internal control and accountability procedures to monitor ethical standards; appraisal, promotion and reward systems that support ethical behaviour. Elsewhere, there have been attempts to shift performance criteria in 'public enterprises' such as state-owned utilities beyond narrow economic efficiency measures to include what Florio (2013, p. 147) terms 'public interest goals', which include 'equity, participation, quality of service, accountability, transparency, quality of the workplace, sustainability, solidarity, public ethos'. The implication is that, even under public ownership, it should not be assumed that foundational providers will meet broader social objectives (which, as Florio notes, now make them more vulnerable to privatisation).

The procedural concerns of the Committee on Standards in Public Life are not trivial, since they impinge on the way employees and clients are treated. But we need to move beyond the general and procedural to a more precise set of activity-specific requirements for privatised utilities, outsourc-ing companies and long-established private providers like supermarkets. The starting point for any debate must be a recognition that, like the old royal monopolies of Charles I and Louis XIV, the corporates here act under a licence from the state, and the terms of that licence must be settled, as would any constitutional arrangement, by public debate. Our proposal is to use social licence to modernise the constitution of monopoly and tie it to the character of the foundational economy.

The notion of 'social licence' is most familiar in the mining industry, particularly in the developing world. It involves a formal or informal agreement between a community and an extractive mining company, which needs the acceptance and approval of the communities in which it operates.[4] The agreement may cover labour conditions, environmental standards, the sharing of economic benefits and other locally important concerns such as the protection of sacred sites. Social licensing in mining was defensively adopted by an industry distrusted by stakeholders and threatened by opposition groups and has often been contained at local community level. Its subsequent history shows that it is not a policy fix but a work in progress, which depends on community social capital and the political articulation of demands by networks of stakeholders at regional and national levels necessary to formulating a collaborative developmental agenda (Owen and Kemp 2013).

Our proposal is that something comparable to the more formal version of a mining social licence be applied to the privatised utilities and giant outsourcers. This would not be a magic fix but a first step in redressing the balance between corporate rights and duties in the foundational economy, which would need to be fitted in to the new politics sketched in the next chapter.

We work by analogy. The extractive industries seek immobile natural resources, but so too do private sector outsourcers that tap tax revenues, and utilities that gain territorial monopolies. The whole franchise system in the foundational economy gives firms the privilege of extracting resources. These resources can come from the taxpayer, as with tax-funded contracts to deliver free-at-point-of-consumption public services; or from a mix of taxation and charges, as with rail franchising; or simply from selling products, as with the privileged position of large supermarkets when planning regulations prevent competitors opening next door. In all these cases, as in mining, one or a few operators gain de facto monopolies and the right to extract from a site or a region.

How might social licensing work in outsourcing? Foundational businesses need to earn the right to extract cash from a state in the form of fees for service and from a population in the form of charges such as rail fares. How might they do so? Here are three core proposals.

- First, licensing would be an explicit arrangement that gave contracting enterprises or sectors privileges and rights to trade, whilst placing them under reciprocal obligations to offer social returns (above and beyond direct provision of a service). A formal licensing system would make the right to trade dependant on providing a service plus meeting negotiated criteria of community responsibility on issues such as sourcing, training and payment of living wages.
- Second, licensing would also be an explicit arrangement governing not only the employment practices and supply contracts of firms (something that has interested the UK's Committee on Standards in Public Life) but which would also address a critical feature, their financial practices. There should, for example, be limits on the use of debt finance, which is too often used to avoid tax at a cost of added fragility in debt-burdened operating businesses.
- Third, the scale and scope of licensing agreements would vary. They might be with whole sectors, including all the firms above a certain size threshold. In other cases, where firm size and market position varied greatly within a sector, it might be more appropriate to have separate firm agreements. Note how flexible and open-ended this suggestion is.

The reasoning behind these proposals is straightforward. The privately owned and operated public monopolies have a sheltered existence – and rightly so, because they deliver services fundamental to the modern state, to modern citizenship, and indeed to civilised life: utilities, welfare services, management of security and justice. They deserve shelter from the instabilities resulting from the gale of competition that rages in so much of a modern economy. But the corollary is that outsourcing cannot simply be about economic transactions, and the contracts under which it operates cannot simply be determined by bottom-line accounting. Outsourcing is about reciprocal social relations within local, regional and national spaces.

The proposal is thus for an extension of government, and indeed for a reframing of the constitution, which is unthinkable as long as firms are conceived to be 'little republics', in the phrase used by Gamble and Kelly (2001). But it is also a very modest proposal. It does not necessarily seek to reverse the outsourcing revolution of recent decades by returning completely to state delivery of public services. It accepts that private corporate actors, SMEs and not-for-profit organisations have a key role in the modern state – indeed, so key that they are best considered governing institutions joined in relations of co-dependence with the state. But it does require that corporate and non-corporate actors so central to delivering foundational services be brought under the constitution with obligations on all sides recognised.

The emphasis here is on a constitutional settlement. Like any constitutional settlement in a democratic state it needs to be freely negotiated; all important actors, corporate and non-corporate, need to have their voices heard and their interests defended. Firms engaged in outsourcing should not be made an offer they cannot refuse. As important partners with the state they are invited to sit down to work out whether and how they can deliver on their social obligations in return for their privileges. That will not be easy, but then democratic constitutional settlements are not meant to be easy: they are meant to be the way we govern in a civilised manner. Naturally, the particular terms of the settlement will vary in different parts of the economy, and naturally once the constitutional silence has been broken, different voices will express different views. But that is what democratic control of economic life should be all about.

A moral and political enterprise

From the beginning, the foundational economy has been an enterprise that dealt in mundane things for elevated ends. The creation of that economy has transformed human lives and enlarged human capabilities – whether we consider clean water, public transport, human education or health and personal care. Viewed from an earlier historical vantage point, it has sometimes looked like an experience of inevitable evolutionary development, as societies learn to combine collective provision with dazzling technological innovation. But the experience is anything but seamlessly evolutionary. At every step of the way there have been 'headwinds', to use Gordon's (2016) polite formulation.

The greatest headwinds have been experienced in the last generation and are domonstrated in the grim record outlined in Chapter 3. The social purpose of the foundational economy has been comprehensively subverted by privatisation and outsourcing, which install high-return business models and opportunistic financial engineering within opaque networks resistant to democratic accountability. The argument in this chapter has been designed to start the job of reinstating the foundational economy as a moral enterprise. But moral purpose plus social licence is not enough. We need some credible ways to counter 'headwinds': in short, some workable political strategies. That is the purpose of the final chapter.

Notes

1 Details of the Well Being of Future Generations (Wales) Act 2015 can be found at: https://futuregenerations.wales/wp-content/uploads/2017/01/150623-guide-to-the-fg-act-en.pdf (accessed 8 February 2018).
2 See, for example, Amsden (1989), Wade (1990) and Yeung (2016).
3 This argument is elaborated in Johal, Moran and Williams (2016).
4 See, for example, discussion of the 'social licence to operate' at: www.miningfacts.org/communities/what-is-the-social-licence-to-operate/ (accessed 8 February 2018).

5 Renewing the foundational

The streets have been paved, and roads now connect all places; houses shelter virtually everyone; the dread diseases are virtually gone, clean water is piped into nearly every building; sanitary sewers carry waste from them; schools and hospitals serve virtually every district; and so on. The accomplishments of the past century in these respects have been truly phenomenal, however short of some persons' aspirations they might have been. But now these relatively easy problems have been dealt with, we have been turning our attention to others that are much more stubborn. (Horst Rittel and Melvin Webber (1973, p. 156))

Foundational renewal as a wicked problem

Rittel and Webber's classic article of 1973 introduced the idea of 'the wicked problem': one that is hard to define, has no set rules for a solution, and yields no one best solution. By way of contrast, benign problems are definable, understandable and yield one consensually acceptable solution. These authors were writing for urban planners and social policy technocrats, inducted into a rationalist conception of science and engineering problem-solving as analytic and sequential. As the opening quotation shows, Rittel and Webber wrote from what might be termed an *end of history* position on what we call the foundational economy: they assumed that all the infrastructure had been built and the material problems of urban life had been solved. Hence the assertion that in the 1970s planners and policymakers would be moving on to tackle trickier problems in different domains.

This triumphalism was premature. We now have a degraded foundational economy occupied by extractive predators, and renewing the foundational is itself a major wicked problem. The word renewal is easy to understand because it conveys the double meaning of repair and of resumption after interruption; it also usefully differentiates foundational renewal, which supports social consumption, from property-led regeneration, which creates asset values for individual benefit. But the problem of foundational renewal is wicked because addressing the questions of how and where to start on renewal are uniquely difficult tasks. The challenge is to turn this book's moral argument about human flourishing and capabilities, and its political argument about citizenship, into an economic and political practice that overcomes obstacles and delivers better access to foundational economy goods and services.

Raymond Williams, who provides the book's opening quote on 'making hope possible', would not have been discouraged by this challenge. He wrote about culture and society from a radical political tradition, where very little is simple and sequential, and closure is usually a false solution. From this political point of view, the radical's task is, then, to 'make hope possible'. With this in mind, the aims of this chapter are straightforward. They are not to prescribe definitions and solutions but to be clearer about the issues around foundational renewal, the nature of the difficult large transition required, and the possibility of constructive first steps. Our argument in this chapter is developed in three sections.

The first section describes the current revival of interest in 'universal basic' income, infrastructure and services. It shows how new problem definitions and innovative policy proposals about universal entitlements are beginning to change established ways of thinking about issues related to the foundational. But we will argue that these interventions, by the Social Prosperity Network and others, also blur the way problems are defined; just as the case of Welsh politics shows how the language of the foundational can be appropriated in a conservative way by those (consciously or not) concerned to defend old ways of policy thinking.

By contrast, in the second section we lay out our own vision of foundational renewal and radical solutions that start with four key shifts in the practice of policy: ask citizens about their foundational priorities; extend social influence over business by a kind of licensing of corporate business, while encouraging small and medium-sized enterprise; reinvent taxation to secure foundational revenue and capital investment; and, finally, create hybrid political alliances for change to drive public policy because government is not always benign or capable. These four changes can also be understood as the preconditions of paradigm shift because they would altogether disrupt top-down policymaking agendas and 'business friendly' policies while at the same time refinancing the state and recognising the limits of government as we know it.

The third and final section takes us to next steps and argues that everyday practice can begin to make hope practical. In the world as it is, change will not begin with some miraculous alignment of our four preconditions. But radical change does not wait for this kind of utopia. We do not have to ask permission to start a local foundational experiment tomorrow, from which can come learning and political mobilisation that begins to create the preconditions.

Progressive thinking and conservative temptation

Official policy thinking, of the kind analysed in Chapter 2, is trapped in contradictions. On the one hand the master problem is to revive growth of GDP but growth is faltering because of deep-seated problems about the rate of productivity increase. There are also widely recognised problems about the distribution of income gains when growth does occur, as well as concerns about ecological sustainability. The position of an elite official body like the Organisation for Economic Co-operation and Development (OECD) embodies these contradictions. It accepts that economic growth is not an end in itself and argues for 'inclusive growth', but nevertheless continues to recommend 'pro-growth structural reforms' without considering whether they might not be part of the problem in the Anglo-Saxon countries (OECD 2014, p. 4).

The wider discussion of inclusive growth now serves as a kind of economic comfort blanket for the policymaking classes. This term is used loosely so that, for example, the OECD and Asian Development Bank definitions are at odds with each other (CAFOD 2014, p. 4). It is hard to argue against the aspiration for less inequality and a broader understanding of human development where growth is a means – and not the only means – rather than an end. But this aspiration will not be realised when policymakers do not recognise the structural drivers of inequality in our financialised capitalism or propose policies adequate to changing a trajectory which steadily disadvantages labour. In parallel, the intense concern with the 'productivity problem' in economies like the UK and Italy proceeds on the unreal assumption that efficiency gains from higher productivity will be broadly distributed to labour.

In macro terms, the underlying problem is a decline in labour's share of GDP, which has fallen by 10% in most OECD countries since the 1970s, in parallel with a skewing of employment rewards to the graduate middle classes. This is caused by globalised low-wage competition and the collapse of high pay, large workplaces and unionised factory employment; all of which is likely to get worse in the next phase, with automation, autonomous cars and such like. In the UK, the bottom 20% of working (non-retired) households have claimed a negligible share of nominal income increases since 1979, while the top 20% claim nearly half. Against this background, the problem is that many of those who talk of inclusive growth will not contemplate re-engineering the power balance in the economy through, for example, re-empowering organised labour. Equally, they do not recommend radical redistribution of incomes through a reshaping of taxation, such as raising income tax rates to allow a significant reduction in value added or sales taxes, which are a regressive tax on consumption.

On the other hand, there is already something approaching a social panic about the prospect of job loss with automation, and widespread alarm about the precarious nature of many of the jobs we do now have. The panic started in elite US institutions like MIT with alarmist books such as Brynjolfsen and McAfee (2011); Oxford's Frey and Osborne (2013) added a sober academic prediction that 47% of US jobs were at risk of computerisation; while McKinsey Global Institute (2017) has made equally apocalyptic predictions about global 'work activities' at risk. The predictions of futurologists are notoriously unreliable. But, in the aggregate, nothing in our capitalism guarantees the compensating creation of new jobs equal to or larger than the number displaced by automation. Much in the history of market economies suggests that social groups displaced by automation will not be able to gain access to new forms of employment; in this case, it is unlikely that many of the new jobs would go to those displaced from activities like bricks and mortar retailing or taxi driving.

The social panic is forcing a rethink by many, including some on the edges of mainstream policymaking. For a variety of reasons (including mediocre growth rates) policymakers are moving on from the idea that average income per capita in GDP or GVA[1] terms is the only (or most important) indicator of well-being. Some policy thinkers and makers are reviving interest in Richard Titmuss' notion of social welfare as a set of minimum standards for all citizens, rather than residual provision for a minority (Titmuss 1950; 1958). This is indicated by the way in which 'universal basic' has become a new catch phrase: thus, we have not just experiments in *universal basic income* in Finland and the Netherlands but also, as discussed below, proposals in the UK for *universal basic infrastructure* and *universal basic services*. And new thinking is also seeping into regional policy. Politically, Wales provides an interesting test case because here, for the first time anywhere in Europe, foundational language is being incorporated into official policy.

Two cheers for these developments. They are welcome progressive shifts, which are broadening the possibilities of policy intervention. But they also bring blurred problem definitions and show how difficult it is to break with the old 'jobs and growth' ways of thinking. So, they are not shifting policy far enough and fast enough to curb the deepening disillusion of European citizens.

Universal basic income proposes giving a basic income from tax revenue to all citizens without means test or employment conditions (Standing 2017; Widerquist 2013), and can be technically implemented through negative income tax or other means. The proposal attracts wide interest, partly because it is ambiguous about the problem it might solve. More precisely, universal basic income solves different problems for the libertarian right and the radical left or feminists, for social welfare policy reformers of all kinds and centrists. For tech entrepreneurs, like Elon Musk, basic income is enlightened self-interest because it promises to make a jobless world safe for the likes of Amazon and Uber (Clifford 2016); while for the centrist Robert Reich (2015), it is about making this world tolerable for the jobless. For radicals and feminists, basic income can be an emancipatory release from wage slavery and fixed gender roles, so we can be more creative and caring; while policy wonks can recommend basic income as a technical fix to simplify the administration of social security.

The fact that universal basic income means so many different things should make us pause but not prevent us from recognising its redistributive potential. In our unequal societies, basic income can weaken the connection between labour market participation and income. This could help carers and many others now in poverty, and it could lessen the disadvantages of taxi drivers and others displaced by automation in the next generation. At the same time, basic income can be used to simplify complex benefits systems, which generate high rates of marginal taxation. But the overall effects of basic income do then depend on how the relation between benefits and wages is engineered. The key issue here is whether basic income is accompanied by corollary policies which enforce minimum wages and conditions and more positively aim for living wages; without such action, basic income easily becomes an incentive for employers to pay sub-standard wages which will be topped up by the state.

At this point, the argument gets lost in arithmetic about basic income levels and affordability. Existing pilot experiments in the Netherlands and Finland sometimes involve conditionality and always offer very low levels of basic income: the current Finnish pilot study offers just €560 unconditionally per month, which is below 20% of median full-time earnings.[2] After considering the UK Green Party's 2015 proposals, John Kay has argued that there is an underlying dilemma here, because either the benefit is too low or the scheme is 'impossibly expensive': in the UK, France and Germany, he calculates that an increase of basic income to 40% of median earnings for all citizens (including children) would require 'all existing tax rates to be increased by more than 20 percentage points' (Kay 2017, p. 72).

Kay's arithmetic is not conclusive because his findings are as much an argument for reform of European national tax systems as they are an argument against basic income. But unconditional, universal income entitlement is expensive and, if taxation is to be reformed, it is not clear why we should give away all the extra revenue raised as income for citizens. The fundamental problem is that basic income jettisons one received idea that jobs are the means of getting income. But basic income persists with another idea which has been a staple of 'market choice' policy reform in recent decades – that we should give citizens income so they can buy welfare through individual consumption. Universal basic income ignores the broader conditions of flourishing, which require the provision of foundational services, and all the social overhead capital expenditure that entails. Any commitment to basic income would therefore need to be balanced with a clear commitment to renewal of foundational services.

The recent UK proposals for universal basic infrastructure and universal basic services do indeed recognise that income is not enough. 'Universal basic infrastructure' is proposed in the final report of the Industrial Strategy Commission. Their focus is on 'the UK's existing hard infrastructure' – rail, energy, water and flood defence, fixed and mobile broadband and fibre – where investment is needed (Industrial Strategy Commission 2017, p. 50). Universal basic services are proposed by a group of University College London researchers in the Social Prosperity Network. In their list, they include four more clearly social services: housing, where a large expansion through new build would double the stock of social housing to 3 million units; transport in the form of free bus travel; free meals for 2.2 million households 'most at risk of food insecurity'; and free communications via phone, internet and BBC TV licence (Social Prosperity Network 2017, p. 12).

The shift from income to infrastructure and services and the emphasis on universal basic entitlement are both significant and welcome. These interventions by the Industrial Strategy Commission and the Social Prosperity Network mark important developments in the debates about infrastructure policy and public service provision, so they deserve close attention. And it is when we give them close attention that some difficulties emerge. In essence, the problems they address are blurred and ill-defined; as a result, it is unclear why they include some systems and services, and exclude others; equally, they do not engage with the crucial issue of the business models that existing providers of these services now use, and new providers would adopt. By reflecting on these issues, we can refine our own problem definition and set up a clear point of departure for the more radical analysis in the next section.

Both reports propose a short list of four systems or services which will become the focus of new investment or expanded service provision. But the full range of providential and material systems and services is much longer and this raises a series of questions: on the selection principle, why some services are included and others excluded; how technical and political decision making fit into the setting of priorities; how costs are to be recovered; and, related to this, what kind of business model is to be prescribed for providers, as prescribed it must be if inappropriate high-risk, high-return models are not to spread further. Some of these questions are not addressed at all by the Industrial Strategy Commission and the Social Prosperity Network; others are answered, but in a way, that discloses a very narrow view of what is universal and basic and how it might be decided.

Thus the Industrial Strategy Commission is true to its brief and adopts a narrow view of infrastructure – rail, broadband etc. – as what builds capabilities for economic development: 'everywhere in the UK should be served by high quality hard infrastructure and have high quality human capital-building universal services' (2017, p. 6). The Social Prosperity Network takes an altogether broader view of basic services. Their report cites Roberto Unger's objective of 'a larger life for the ordinary person'.[3] But this objective is then interpreted in a very narrow way. It is not clear why, for example, adult care is excluded or the underfunding of current health services is not addressed; and two of their four services (social housing and free meals) are neither universal nor majoritarian because provision is explicitly to be focused on those in the bottom income deciles. In other words, they are not basic universal services at all.

It will be plain that in respect of these two important sets of proposals, the devil lies in the detail. And that detail will be decided politically – in other words by struggles within and around government. Thus it is crucial, though unclear, who decides and at what level which sectors are given priority; who adjudicates on the investment and operating subsidy claims of different sectors; or who determines the resourcing of different regions. The working assumption of both reports seems to be that the political classes involved in policymaking – experts, civil servants, office holding politicians – should be trusted to choose from a menu of choices. The Industrial Strategy Commission wants to loosen up funding constraints with a Public Investment Bank and a broadening of project appraisal techniques, but otherwise has little to say on hard choices. The Social Prosperity Network report simply recommends 'more devolved local government, capable of providing responsive and accountable service design and development' (2017, p. 15). Both reports assume government at all levels is benign and competent, and that issues about citizen disengagement, civic gain or deficit, or regional identity do not need to be discussed.

What might be called real capitalist issues about cost recovery, pricing policies and business models are equally neglected. The Industrial Strategy Commission report works on the assumption that the problem is levering in investment and getting projects built; so, for example, there is no discussion of whether system-wide fares should be set to recover operating costs on railways, nor of how public transport fares should be varied to meet social objectives in low density areas or at peak times. The Social Prosperity Network solves the pricing problem by extending the NHS principle and insisting that all its universal basic services should be free-at-point-of-use: most notably 1.5 million new social housing units will be allocated 'on a needs basis at zero rent' which means rent free, no council tax, and with a utilities allowance. On this basis, free-at-point-of-use dramatically limits the number of services that can be provided beyond health and schooling (which are already free), and creates dilemmas about policy for services like residential care, which are expensive and are, usually for that reason, part charged and part free-at-point-of-use.

These vital neglected issues are not just technical or procedural – they determine the viability of the proposals. And
a further series of questions arises about what business models
are appropriate and how new universal basic services will be
owned and organised. In a very traditional way, neither the
Industrial Strategy Commission nor the Social Prosperity
Network confront the business models which lead to the
wrecking of the foundational economy, as described in Chapter
3 of this book. The Industrial Strategy Commission recognises
discontent with privatised utilities but then suggests that
regulatory reform should take the form of creating a single
regulator lodged in the Competition and Markets Authority
(2017, p. 57). In other words, it responds to a generation of
failure to make the market work by proposing a piecemeal
institutional reform designed to make the market work. It
encourages economists to continue hunting the snark of
competitive markets. Outsourcing to least-cost providers with
high-return business models – the poison in the system, as we
showed earlier – is not explicitly discussed in either report.
The Social Prosperity Network does not consider who will
be providing their universal services so that, for example,
there is no bar on Sodexo or G4S opening kitchens to supply
a large number of free meals. Under these conditions, universal
basic services would effectively open up new fields of opportunity for the outsourcing conglomerates.

There is, then, real and encouraging change in the way
the workings of public services are being discussed in the
proposals for universal basic infrastructure and services. But
the new discussion of universal basics is marked with silences
and contradictions. While trying to think out some way of
escaping the problems of growing inequality and inadequate
services and infrastructure, these reports are trapped inside
the intellectual and institutional world of metropolitan elites
who will make choices for their citizens. These reports do
not recognise that the foundational renewal problem is about
centralised, top-down policymaking as much as it is about
the wrong policies.

The possibilities and difficulties of escaping this world are illustrated by recent developments in policymaking by regional government in Wales. The context here is the perceived failure of mainstream economic policies in a deindustrialised laggard region. The aim of devolved Welsh government in the late 1990s was to close the GVA gap with London and the South East; but after twenty years, the ratios have not shifted at all. There is a small policy community in Cardiff with radicals in unexpected places like the Welsh Federation of Small Businesses and in the Housing Associations, as well as within the ranks of Assembly Members. Hence a Welsh Assembly debate on the foundational economy in Wales in early 2017 and a Welsh minister for the economy who name checks 'foundation sectors' in his Action Plan (Welsh Government 2017d, p. 15). But significantly, what we have in Welsh policy so far is a new language, along with more blurred problem definitions and an elision of old and new ways of thinking.

The Welsh discussion of the foundational economy usefully shifts the attention of regional policymakers away from the obsession with 'next-generation industries', which national policymakers based in London are still sponsoring in Wales and other UK regions through policies like the Swansea Bay city deal signed in 2017 (Earle *et al.* 2017). This is a progressive shift because it engages with the regional economy as it is, rather than how policymakers would like it to be. So Welsh policy can now engage with hitherto neglected sectors like social care; though it is not yet clear what is to be done about such a sector in terms of re-organisation. Beyond the new focus on hitherto neglected sectors, there is new thinking by regional policymakers in their discussion of place-based policies for problem areas. However, this is mixed up with old preoccupations; as in the report of the Valleys Task Force, which plans some sensible interventions like a social care provider business network but also insists 'the number of jobs in the foundational economy will be increased' (Welsh Government 2017c, pp. 7, 21). Of course, Wales does need more and better jobs, but a foundational agenda should mean policy aims well beyond just getting people into work in sectors like social care.

We welcome progressive developments, like the idea of universal basic services proposed by academics, or the interest in the foundational economy from Welsh policymakers, because they recognise the need for new thinking and can establish a base for further movement. More generally, these developments are not enough, fundamentally because they presume that – at national or regional level – policy means the choice of the political classes put into effect by a willing and able state apparatus. But everything in the preceding chapters of this book shows that, over the last generation, retreating states have, through failure to control privatisation and outsourcing, licensed the disorganisation of the foundational economy and extraction by those with high-return business models. Something more radical is needed that addresses the limits of this model of policymaking, the character of this state and the way that state incapacity and corporate predation are both outside the field of the visible for metropolitan and regional elites. The next section outlines four key shifts that are designed to accomplish this.

A radical vision of four key shifts

Our vision starts from what we could call the European question: if we live in high-income, wealthy societies, why do so many of our citizens have stunted lives? And why, beyond the here and now, are we so careless about the welfare of future generations or populations outside our enclave of privilege? At the heart of this stunting is a problem about limited foundational entitlements. For example, European citizens in towns and cities need more than an income. They need a decent dwelling as a home base for a fulfilled life, with the house's system connections set in an environment of parks, libraries and transport systems. The dwelling is essential regardless of income, and the surrounding systems and connections cannot be fixed by giving people income for individual consumption in a marketplace.

And failure of foundational provision in areas like housing is a matter not of economic inevitability but of political logic. The system provision is not one about productive constraint; it is about political priorities and distribution in European societies which are both resource abundant and resource profligate. When we were so much poorer in the 1950s, we could afford old-age pensions, libraries and free hospitalisation, so why can we not afford adult care now? Problems like the funding of adult care will not be solved by redistributing consumer income but by political action to create new entitlements backed by material systems provision, including imaginative building of community centres and homes. As argued in Chapter 4, if we cannot sort entitlements for citizens within our territory here and now, we have little chance of doing anything for future generations and excluded groups.

There is also a huge opportunity to pursue environmental responsibility as a collective, social good. At present, environmental responsibility is too often represented as a puritan individual consumption choice which (in a society of hedonists) will most likely appeal to a socially aware minority, while it alienates many citizens and easily becomes regressive. Consider the contribution of air transport to global warming or the specific problem of motor vehicles and air pollution where, according to the European Environment Agency (2017, p. 9), particulates and nitrous oxides in 2014 caused 374,000 premature deaths in the EU 28. Cheap European flights are part of the larger life of ordinary people for most of the 129 million passengers Ryanair carried in 2017.[4] Equally, congestion charging, higher general taxes on motoring and restrictions on car use will have regressive impacts in car-dependent cities where their effect would be to limit economic and social participation by low income groups who make up the motoring poor.

From this point of view, foundational thinking takes environmental responsibility seriously, arguing the effort must go into redesigning the systems that underpin social consumption. We agree wholeheartedly with Kate Raworth's (2017) argument in *Doughnut Economics* that the aim is to secure the 'social foundation' of essentials like food, housing and healthcare without damaging 'Earth's life supporting systems' through global warming and environmental degradation. What foundational thinking adds is the idea that how we go about providing that social foundation (through systems for social access) is important in itself, and that renewed provision requires prior critical analysis of corporate business models and practices of policymaking. With these additions, new foundational systems and changes in policymaking are the systemic key to safeguarding the social foundation while curbing environmental damage.

The foundational proposal is thus for systems-based redistribution which expands universal entitlement to services. For that we need a new political and economic practice which, in turn, requires a series of major shifts that positively change the paradigm of what policy can be and negatively removes blockages and constraints. The passages below explain the four shifts already summarised in this chapter's introduction: end top-down agendas by simply asking citizens about their foundational priorities; end 'business friendly' as a euphemism for corporate predation and introduce a truly business friendly regime which extends social influence over business, and gives it more legitimacy by licensing corporate business and supporting small business; re-finance the state by reinventing taxation; and, finally, recognise that government is often not benign or competent by creating new hybrid political alliances for change.

Shift 1: Ask citizens what they want so that foundational policy can come out of a conversation, not a top-down agenda

On the demand side of the foundational economy, we can start with a statement of the blindingly obvious: foundational interventions should begin by asking citizens what they want, and by building up a knowledge base about their foundational priorities as well as a map of existing foundational provision. In the nineteenth century, gas and water had a self-evident utility and protective function because cholera kills and Weisbach's incandescent mantle, like Edison's carbon filament lamp, effectively extended day light. But when European cities and regions now have a multiplicity of foundational services and fragmented societies, citizen preferences cannot be taken for granted and must be discovered before they can input into policymaking.

If asking citizens about foundational priorities is elementary common sense, it would also change the world taken for granted by most of Europe's political classes and their expert helpers. They are accustomed to more anodyne forms of 'public consultation' about operating detail when all the major decisions have been taken on transport systems, urban property re-development and such like. And any shift from the rituals of public consultation would also be highly disruptive because there is a large priorities gap between well-meaning top-down policy agendas and the expressed priorities of citizens. That much is suggested in the UK case by national surveys like the Populus survey of September 2017 reported by the Legatum Institute (Elliott and Kanagasooriam 2017) and by city region surveys like the People's Plan Greater Manchester (2017) or the Welsh Valleys Taskforce, where a government commission asked communities what they want.

The Populus survey used the technique of MaxDiff analysis to establish a hierarchy of priorities about 'utilities and public services'. The hierarchy is established by asking respondents to choose most and least important from a constantly changing list of three or four options (the ranking then emerges without asking respondents directly to rank 20 services). Exhibit 5.1 presents the survey results for all respondents and then for sub-groups of respondents differentiated by gender, age and social class. The results are fascinating in several ways. When it comes to high priority, absolutely essential services and

Exhibit 5.1 Populus survey of UK service priorities

| | Priority for all respondents | Breakdown of responses by: | | | | | | |
| | | Gender | | Age | | | Social grade | |
		Male	Female	18–24	65+	AB	DE
Food and water	1	1	1	1	1	1	1
Emergency services	2	2	2	3	2	2	2
Universal healthcare	3	3	3	2	3	3	3
A good house	4	4	4	4	4	4	4
A decent well-paying job	5	5	5	5	6	5	5
Compulsory & free education	6	6	6	6	7	6	7
Armed Forces	7	7	7	10	5	7	6
Ability to save funds/bank	8	8	8	9	8	8	9

Minimum wage	9	9	9	7	11	9	8
Further & higher education	10	10	10	8	14	10	11
Large supermarkets	11	13	11	12	13	13	10
Television & radio	12	11	12	16	9	11	12
Your own car	13	12	14	17	10	12	15
Internet and search engines	14	14	15	11	15	15	13
Books	15	15	13	13	12	14	14
Subsidised public transport	16	16	16	14	16	16	16
Smart devices	17	17	17	15	17	17	17
The arts	18	18	18	18	18	18	18
Affordable air travel	19	19	19	19	19	19	19
Social media platforms	20	20	20	20	20	20	20

Note: The data is based on a poll of 2,004 UK members of the public carried out by Populus in August 2017 using a Max-Diff technique, where respondents were asked to choose the most and least important services from a changing subset of the 20 services listed in the table.

Source: Elliott and Kanagasooriam (2017, p. 56).

utilities, the foundational priorities of UK citizens might be described as classical. Sub-group differences then emerge mainly about lower order priorities. And overall, there is a clear priorities gap between citizens and policymakers, mainstream and radical.

In order of descending priority, the top six services are: food and water, emergency services, universal healthcare, a good house, a decent well-paying job and compulsory free education. Four of these six top priorities are nineteenth century innovations, and healthcare free-at-point-of-use is part of the post-war settlement. Internet and search engines do not make the top ten and affordable air travel and social media platforms come bottom of the table at numbers 19 and 20. From a different point of view, this reinforces Robert Gordon's (2016) productivity-based arguments about the significance of late nineteenth-century innovation. What we can see is that these innovations did more than boost productivity in the eighty years up to 1970; they are of enduring quasi epochal significance because (with healthcare) these are the things that still matter to citizens now. Differences of gender, age, class and party affiliation have very little effect on the ranking of top priorities: most groups are near enough agreed on these. The generational and political differences come in the ranking of lower order priorities: as when, for example, young respondents are much less enamoured of car ownership.

Just as important, from a foundational point of view, there is a clear priorities gap between citizen priorities and mainstream or radical policymaker agendas.

- Jobs and skills training are the superordinate objectives of mainstream policy. But 'a decent well-paid job' comes in as priority number five after universal healthcare and a good house at numbers three and four; skills and training represented by further and higher education come in around number ten, well behind free schooling.

- If we shift to consider policy innovation, free local transport is one of the five free 'universal basic services' advocated by the UCL researchers whose work we discussed above. But 'subsidised public transport' comes in as priority number sixteen for all respondents; and, even 18–24 year olds (who are less interested in owning a car) rate subsidised public transport no higher than number 14.

Of course, citizen priorities in a national poll are very abstract and general. In specific cities and regions, the choices will be more specific and focused. But similar basic priorities and the same worrying priorities gap between citizens and policymakers emerges from local surveys like the People's Plan Greater Manchester, the Valleys Taskforce in Wales and other local evidence.

Policymakers have, through planning permissions since the 1990s, facilitated the rebuilding of Manchester's city centre, which has expanded the housing stock with one- or two-bedroom buy-to-let flats rented mainly by young professionals. But respondents to an online questionnaire wanted more family housing for the 80,000 on the waiting list for social housing in Greater Manchester. The Greater Manchester Spatial Framework, published by policymakers in autumn 2016, envisages that economic growth over the next twenty years will require large-scale new build of apartments in the city centre and houses in edge of city developments; this Spatial Framework does not once mention the word 'social housing' (GMCA 2016).

In Wales, the Valleys Taskforce highlights the priorities gap in a rather different way. This is a government-led project to develop a plan for a sub region – *Our Valleys, Our Future* – where the coal mines have closed and factories have shut. Through a variety of engagement activities, the taskforce sought citizen views about what matters to them and how they would like to see their community improved. The policymakers approached engagement with their preoccupation about jobs and income, while citizen respondents consistently told them that other things like public services, public transport and open spaces were just as valuable and should be improved. Alongside 'good quality jobs and the skills to do them', two of the three citizen priorities were 'better public services' and 'my community' (Welsh Government 2017a, p. 6; Welsh Government 2017b).

Nobody would claim that the Populus survey, the Manchester People's Plan or the Valleys Taskforce engagements give us a definitive picture of what the priorities of citizens are for the foundational economy. But they do highlight gaps between popular and elite priorities, which show that we need a much more effective toolkit to allow us to find out what groups of citizens in specific places do want. And that incidentally would take us further away from any kind of nanny state because citizen priority questions should be about the background systems which allow citizens to secure their own conceptions of the good life.

The established mechanisms of political decision making – which involve crude choices offered by party competition coupled with delegation of authority over choices to experts – just do not allow the expression of popular priorities on foundational provision. Surveys of the Populus type have obvious limitations; but equally, we now have many other established means of exploring citizen priorities, including citizen juries and focus groups. Policymakers also need to develop and draw on new tools like foundational surveys which would allow citizens at different scales to become aware of and articulate their foundational deficits. The aim of such surveys would be to highlight the areas (like housing in Greater Manchester) where there are shared problems about access to, and quality of, foundational goods and services in a specific community. This would give voice to the community, build collective consciousness of shared problems, and empower action.

The results would become input for doing policy with and for communities; not doing policy to communities according to elite preferences. This need not displace experts and representative democracy with plebiscites and referenda. The point is not that, as Michael Gove argued in the Brexit referendum, the people have had enough of experts. The people cannot do without experts and politicians, but they have a lot to learn about how responsibly to explore citizen priorities and integrate those priorities into policymaking. A knowledge of those priorities is an essential element in policymaking; it would reduce the likelihood of policymakers editing out what they do not want to hear.

Shift 2: Extend social influence over business by adopting social licensing for all large corporates (public, not-for-profit and private) and mapping small and medium enterprises (SMEs) and micro businesses to build their capabilities

On the supply side of the foundational economy, businesses are an asset. In finance texts, an asset is classically defined as something useful which is owned or controlled; in the case of foundational business (whether public, not-for-profit or privately owned), we might change the descriptor to businesses that are capable and socially influenced. In this frame, the aim of policy is to extend the sphere of social influence and capability by working in a discriminating way on the existing stock of businesses in a regional or national economy.

Ending the 'business friendly' model of policy is sensible because it has achieved so little. This entails scrapping the assumption that business policy is primarily a matter of adding a finance input through investment banks, research and development subventions and such like; or offering financial concessions and incentives to business in the form of lower tax rates and free infrastructure. The question of what policy should do instead is complex, but it should surely be guided by three aims: first, private business enterprise is here to stay in the foundational economy, and therefore it should be given a legitimate place as a provider of essential public services; second, legitimation of large corporates (publicly owned and not-for-profit as well as privately owned) should involve a system of social licensing; and, third, policy should distinguish clearly between different types of business, which will require different policies.

If it is accepted that large public companies, SMEs grounded in a community and often marginal micro firms will all present different challenges and opportunities, then there are separate questions about what can be achieved by reinstating discarded, unfashionable organisational forms like the nationalised corporation; or by promoting alternative organisational models like locally interlinked cooperatives on the Mondragon model. Reinstated and alternative organisational forms are relevant but, in our view, public policy has to start by working with and on the existing stock of firms in a discriminating way. This means putting social restraints on large private firms and building the economic capability of small firms.

There are, of course, gains to be made from influencing public-sector anchor institutions and most of them should do more to improve the well-being of their people and places. For example, anchors like hospitals and universities should be 'living wage' employers; they should promote career progression for the lowest paid, and they should actively use their procurement power, not only to 'buy local' but to build business capability. But the leverage via public-sector anchors is limited when the main spend of such organisations is on employee salaries which are already going into the local community. To get major results from reshaping business behaviour in the foundational economy it is necessary to tackle the larger part of local household spend, which goes through large firms in the private sector, like supermarkets and retail banks and utilities. The proposal for social licensing has already been developed in Chapter 4, so we can briefly illustrate here how social licensing can reshape the behaviour of private firms and offer local communities a potentially powerful set of levers.

Take grocery retailing and supermarkets: as Exhibit 2.3 showed, the average household across the EU 28 spent €86.98 per week on food and non-alcoholic drinks in 2016, much of it in supermarkets. Planning and regulatory systems in the past generation have licensed edge-of-town supermarkets with a local, largely captive market for the extraction of this regular spend from the local community, yet there is almost nothing in the policymaking system which requires supermarkets to 'act local'. There is even less obligation on the next generation of online grocery retailers, who meet demand not from local stores but from regional centres. Acting local could include developing the skills of local populations, selling regional products nationally or taking preventive responsibility for health through diet.[5] This example is important because it underlines how the foundational economy is about more than utilities and public services like water, railways and healthcare. It is about all the institutions that contribute to a fulfilled life and shape the quality of life for citizens.

With SMEs and micro firms, we reach the many firms that are beneath the radar of fund investors and mainstream policymakers. Most SMEs are of little interest to fund investors because they are not growing fast; those which are fast-growing in the UK often become tradeable assets after early sale by a founding owner-manager (Brill *et al.*, 2015, pp. 31–44). Micro firms will mainly be surviving precariously by selling labour hours in activities like construction, or running small retail or food businesses. SMEs are often treated meanly by the banks, but the fix of adding finance through regional institutions or public investment banks is irrelevant to smaller SMEs. These firms cannot easily find the owner-manager's salary and then pay charges for equity or make re-payments on bank loans. In this unknown territory for policy, a first step is to

map local businesses, understand more about capabilities and
the sources of precarity, while focusing on recurrent problems
like early sale by founding families or retirement of older
owner-managers.

Policies for SMEs and micro firms need to be explicitly
experimental. One major objective should be to reduce the
precarity that leads to high death rates among small firms
and makes many averse to any kind of borrowing. This requires
supply-chain interventions which give such firms better access
to demand, for example in the form of smaller contracts or
predictable volumes, as well as prompt payment by larger
firms and organisations. As for building capability, this involves
much more than upskilling workforces, because there is a
need to support management capacity in everything from
accounting to employment law, and to figure out how this
can be done, partly by drawing on the resources of larger
organisations and local business.

This major policy shift to restrain corporate business and
encourage small (often family) business does not involve any
generalised view for or against private for-profit ownership.
The shift does connect with much earlier studies showing a
link between concentrations of SMEs and higher levels of
community well-being (Mills and Ulmer 1946; Lyson 2006).
Much the same point could be made about alternative forms
of ownership like nationalised corporations or mutuals and
co-ops. These alternatives can find a place in a reorganised
foundational economy where, under specific circumstances,
they can be appropriate ways of organising service delivery.
But there is the need to be unsentimental about the scope for
these alternatives when the foundational economy is also
characterised by an ecology of private enterprise, and is likely
to remain so given the expense of extending public ownership
with compensation and the difficulty of creating capable, large
co-operatives. Equally, the issue is not ownership per se but,
firstly, the interaction of ownership and business model in
specific activities and, secondly, whether that contributes to

the only end that matters, creating a foundational economy that leads to fulfilled lives.

Categorically, the state-owned corporation should not be seen as a generic form that solves the problems of delivering foundational services. This kind of integrated organisation is technically well suited to running large, complex, centralised network systems of rail track, pipeline distribution or electricity generation. But distributed systems are possible in many activities, and several providential services present quite different problems. In social care, for example, it would be sensible for the state to borrow cheaply to build care homes which could then be operated on a fee-for-service basis by many different kinds of providers. Furthermore, the state-owned corporation created by nationalisation ends extraction through paying dividends and adding debt, but does not guarantee a sustainable business model. The limits of cost recovery from customers and the sources of investment funding need to be considered if public ownership is not to be discredited by underfunding and operating deficits.

As for co-operatives and mutuals, as argued in Chapter 3, the practices of Italian co-ops in welfare services show how the absence of extraction for capital does not guarantee social virtue, and larger social enterprises need to be subject to social licensing. In the case of the Mondragon federation of co-ops in Spain, that success is significant, though it owes much to specific, unrepeatable conditions. In every European economy small co-ops can help deal with SME problems about owner-families wanting to sell out and owner-managers needing to retire, though there are limits to the role of co-ops as agents of transformation in a re-localised economy, on the basis of existing structures and practices. For example, the Evergreen co-ops in Cleveland, a commonly cited model, have a small base of captive demand from local public anchor institutions; this sustains the local co-ops but they apparently do not have the broad capability to grow to employ significant numbers by expanding into contested areas. After nine years, in 2017 the three Evergreen coops in Cleveland operating in LED lights, laundry and greenhouse-grown lettuce have 140 employees, of whom 60 are co-op members.[6]

As for localisation of production, that makes sense if it is building capability in local firms whose main markets will often then be outside the locality. This was the case in Enfield Borough where an extended experiment was designed to ensure local firms had the certification and skills to insulate social housing (Johal and Williams 2013). But we should not promote post-code localism of the kind which involves counting addresses on supplier invoices and then celebrating success in keeping demand within one locality or region. We have, elsewhere, analysed the weakness of this approach in Wales (Brill *et al.* 2015, pp. 45–57). This kind of Keynesianism within one small region can very easily become simply an autarkic diversion that promotes a stultifying kind of competition between localities and regions, based on creating sheltered reservations rather than building business capability.

Shift 3: Reinvent taxation so that there is a revenue base for foundational services and investment

Right across Europe, the reinvention of taxation is urgent because states are running out of tax revenue to fund providential services and material investment. Austerity states like the UK are struggling to finance current expenditure, and they are not alone. In the UK, in the half century after the mid-1950s, the long-term trend of health expenditure was of real increase at 4.1% per annum; since 2010, the average real increase has been just 1.3% per annum. By 2014–15 the funding gap was such that the NHS was being asked to make efficiency savings of £22 billion by 2020, an unprecedented task for a system which has always provided healthcare for a relatively modest share of GDP.[7]

Just as serious, but less publicised, is the problem of falling levels of public investment in material infrastructure in OECD countries. That is alarming given the huge capital demands of the *Energiwende* or transition to low carbon energy which is projected to cost Germany alone €525 billion by 2025; while Germany and other European countries also face huge bills for sorting broadband fibre to the home. In the EU, public investment, which was running at 3% or more of GDP in the two decades before the financial crisis, had fallen to 2.1% by 2014 (Plank 2016, p. 8). And this is not just the result of austerity cuts in Southern Europe: German public investment is consistently around one third below the EU 28 average in a range of 2–2.5%; and German public investment at the municipal level has been negative since 2003 (Plank 2016, pp. 8–9; Chazan 2017).

We live in rich societies of socially created surpluses: the problem is not scarcity of resources. Rather, it is a problem of whether we have the political will and economic capacity to use that surplus for foundational purposes through reinvention of taxation to fund current expenditure and prudent capital investment in low-risk, long return foundational projects. The problem of political will relates partly to how tax is often represented as a drag on 'enterprise' and is always unpopular with powerful interests that do not want to pay tax. The power of privileged groups, like the rich, and privileged institutions, like corporations, cannot just be willed away, but a start can be made by challenging the biases in language. Tax is not a drag on 'enterprise'; it is a way the state claims a rightful share of surpluses on behalf of the community that helped create those surpluses. These surpluses are socially created in two ways: first through profiting from unearned increases in capital and rental values, classically of land and housing; and second, through declaring corporate profits without deduction of charges for social overhead expenditure for everything from roads to schooling to policing. This last mechanism ensures that much self-styled 'enterprise' relies on foundational services without which social reproduction would collapse.

Innovation is urgent because the existing tax system is regressive and disproportionately hits consumption by lower income groups. The 'thirty glorious years' after the end of the Second World War were underpinned by tax innovations which always were (or increasingly became) regressive. Thus social insurance and post-1945 systems of deducting income tax before wages were paid had a strong element of getting the working class to pay for their own. That was partly redeemed by high nominal rates of income tax on upper income groups. This benefit was always partly notional when high rates bred tax avoidance. But that notional benefit is now lost because the maximum income tax rates across West European countries are all now in a range 45–55%. As for more recent changes, these have been regressive. Value Added Tax was introduced by France in 1954 and then standardised across Europe. This regressive tax on consumption now accounts for up to 20% of state revenues. In contrast, the 34 nations of the OECD currently have an average nominal corporation tax on profits of just 25%.[8] Moreover, for the biggest and most sophisticated businesses the tax is generally optional, because they have the resources – smart lawyers and tax accountants – to develop schemes for avoidance.

What we need is taxes on wealth, especially experiments with land value tax. As Atkinson (2015) and Piketty (2014) have demonstrated, the post-war tax and welfare settlements had a levelling influence, but by the 2010s the high-income countries of North America and Western Europe had returned to pre-1914 levels of income and wealth inequality, and there has been a great rise in the wealth-to-income ratio. As Ryan-Collins, Lloyd and Mcfarlane (2017) have subsequently argued, in the UK the rise in wealth-to-income ratio since 1980 is driven entirely by capital gains, without which it would actually have declined. The largest, most widely dispersed source of capital gains is house property: the value of UK 'dwellings' (houses and land) increased from £1.2 trillion to £5.5 trillion between 1995 and 2015.

But closer examination of the social distribution of different forms of wealth is worthwhile. Exhibit 5.2, based on UK data,

Exhibit 5.2 Distribution of UK household net wealth, 2012–14

Households grouped by wealth	Property wealth (net) (%)	Financial wealth (net) (%)	Physical wealth (%)	Private pension wealth (%)	Total wealth (%)	Total wealth (£m)	Average wealth per household (£)
Decile 1	−0.1	−0.7	1.5	0.0	0.1	5,686	2,219
Decile 2	0.0	0.0	3.8	0.2	0.5	55,086	21,501
Decile 3	0.6	0.3	6.4	0.9	1.3	142,757	55,721
Decile 4	2.7	1.0	7.4	1.9	2.6	292,488	114,253
Decile 5	5.2	1.8	8.6	3.2	4.2	472,923	184,663
Decile 6	8.2	3.1	9.8	4.7	6.2	693,799	270,698
Decile 7	10.8	5.7	11.4	7.5	8.8	980,842	382,693
Decile 8	14.1	9.3	13.0	12.2	12.5	1,394,251	544,842
Decile 9	19.0	15.0	15.5	21.2	18.9	2,107,677	822,669
Decile 10	39.5	64.7	22.6	48.1	44.8	4,988,712	1,947,955
All	100.0	100.0	100.0	100.0	100.0	11,134,221	434,676

Note: Households are grouped into ten deciles according to their total wealth, where decile 1 is the poorest and decile 10 the richest by wealth. Property and financial wealth are shown as net, taking account of any debt. The table shows the percentage of total wealth of different kinds which belongs to the households that make up each of the deciles, as well as the average amount of household wealth.

Source: ONS, Wealth in Great Britain Wave 4: 2012 to 2014, https://www.gov.uk/government/statistics/wealth-in-great-britain-wave-4-2012-to-2014.

brings out two important points about wealth distribution, which apply more broadly across Europe: first, the distribution is skewed not just by the wealth of those in the top 1% or 5% but by the wealth of those in the top 30%, or even the top 50%, which will include many ordinary readers of this book whose only assets are a house and a pension; second, the privileged groups hold a diverse portfolio of assets including financial coupons and pension entitlements as well as house property. In the UK case, if we classify households into deciles by wealth, the top 30% of households own 76% of all wealth and within this total, they own 73% of property wealth, 89% of (net) financial wealth and 82% of private pension wealth, which is separately classified.

It is therefore economically appropriate to focus on capital gains and revive the devices of land tax and death duties advocated by early twentieth-century radicals. It is also politically appropriate to revive their hundred-year-old arguments about how land and property allow private appropriation of socially created wealth. Land value tax already commands some support not just from left progressives but also from free market economists: it has been described as 'the least bad tax' by Milton Friedman, and has been advocated in the UK by the free market think tank the Institute of Economic Affairs.[9] Various groups support the principle of land value taxation for different reasons, of course, but from the point of view of foundational renewal it has two advantages.

- First, it connects to the material foundational economy, created by land use planning policies and by state investment in the physical infrastructure of networked services. Land use planning decisions can create huge windfall gains for landowners, not only as developers but as homeowners or small business operators. Investments in transport infrastructure – think of the impact of new train or tram links – can transform property values. Land value tax signals that the state is willing and able to reclaim some of that gain for public purposes.

- Second, in terms of practicalities, land value tax is relatively hard to avoid, can be designed to be broadly progressive and is not a 'blue sky' idea. So, we can learn from experience of different schemes operating in a range of very different state jurisdictions from Estonia to the US.

Shift 4: Build hybrid foundational alliances with intermediate institutions because government is not always benign or competent

The basic idea here is that public policy on foundational renewal is too important to be left solely to governments in their current (structurally and ideationally) enfeebled condition. Across Europe, there are important differences in national electoral systems, in parliamentary cultures and in administrative traditions. But classically, after 1945, progress was delivered by capturing the central state apparatus, by winning a parliamentary majority for a party programme so that ministers could require administrators to throw the levers of national policy. This is increasingly problematic in many European countries. In some states, like the UK, party systems are fragmenting, destroying the stable majorities that supported programmatically driven governments. In others, like Germany, party elites are losing the capacity to create governing coalitions that can sustain programmes.

Increasingly also, governments do not know what to do at either national or EU level. Thus, in November 2017, the EU held a 'social summit' at Gothenburg, registered the importance of 'real improvement in people's daily lives', stated 20 principles or worthy objectives and (in our view) added nothing new and plausible on how to get there.[10] The generation after 1945 was an age of what Scott (1998) describes as 'high modernism': governments then had grand projects for building everything from the welfare state to supersonic passenger jets. But the trauma of the great financial crisis sucked that kind of confidence out of political leadership. The decade of the 2010s has been dominated by the grinding business of managing austerity and economic underperformance, with the addition of new concepts like 'smart specialisation', and increasing reliance on indirect engagement with the economy through monetary policy.

In the jargon of policymaking, smart specialisation is about place-based strategies, which strengthen innovation to boost productivity and deliver endogenous growth; at the OECD, the argument is that 'countries or regions identify and select a limited number of priority areas for knowledge based investment' (OECD 2013). Like much recent policy, it is produced by a process of remix, which combines old and new ideas from different sources. Specifically, smart specialisation combines old economics-based ideas about comparative advantage with more recent science and policy studies ideas about the importance of supporting early-stage producer investment in innovation; at the EU level, this is slotted into a prescriptive politics about creating a 'business friendly' environment, where government and universities can partner with business. Smart specialisation has been taken up at EU level because it provides a framework within which the EU and national governments can rationalise whatever they want to do, as in the case of the UK.[11] For the EU, the policy licenses much, including (predictably) more support for inter-regional projects in next-generation industries such as 'big data, bio-economy, resource efficiency, connected mobility or advanced manufacturing'.[12]

Much more significant in terms of Europe-wide economic effects, the major policy innovation since 2007 has been zero interest rates and quantitative easing, pursued by the European Central Bank and the national central banks, as policymakers tried to escape the consequence of the great crash. The results of treatment were as bad as the disease: loose monetary policy boosted asset prices and wealth inequality while tight fiscal policy restricted current expenditure and government borrowing for overdue foundational investment. Government reliance on monetary policy involved delegating responsibility for economic management to central banks even though there was no precedent for persisting with such loose monetary policies.

This delegation partly reflected the disabling effects of privatisation and outsourcing on the central state's administrative capability to initiate and manage anything complex. Absence of knowledge and ignorance of consequences is a positive advantage for the wrecking crew breaking up a social settlement. Rail privatisation is a classic case: in the UK it was embarked upon with coarse assertions about self-evident benefits, and justified afterwards with bits of confirming evidence (Moran 2001). More generally, privatisation and outsourcing result in a dismantling of the state's administrative capabilities in planning, project control and operations management. The predictable results include limited capacity to engage with details of policymaking and implementation, and the destruction of the tacit knowledge that accumulates in stable administrative systems.

This process of destruction has gone so far in the UK that there must be questions about whether a Treasury-dominated central state and austerity-weakened local government have the strategic vision and administrative capacity to initiate and manage many of the complex projects that would renew the foundational economy. If we then look across Europe, there is great variation in organisation and capacity. There are obviously substantial differences in formal arrangements, like the degree to which government is organised on federal or unitary lines (contrast Germany and the UK). And there are also obvious differences in the size and capacity of municipalities and the extent of local government's financial dependence on central government. If we look at local tax revenue as a percent of total revenue for the 28 EU countries, for instance, we find substantial variation, with local tax revenues above

50% of total local revenue in Spain, Sweden and Austria, and well below 20% in the UK, Netherlands and Greece, as Exhibit 5.3 shows. And what these variations tell us is that the capacity of the local to get things done varies hugely across Europe.

We note this evidence because the 'local option' is attractive to many progressive defenders of the foundational economy, and its attraction is perhaps enhanced by the very distinguished part played by municipalities in the original building of the material domain through 'gas and water' municipal enterprise. But local government is not automatically more virtuous because 'it brings decision making closer to the people'. As Born and Purcell (2006) argued in their classic article, the effects of localism depend on the policy agenda. And here there is cause for concern about how, in many of Europe's major cities, local government is sponsoring property-led regeneration as the socially meretricious and privately profitable substitute for foundational renewal. The city region governments which built the foundational economy through great projects 100 or so years ago have, since the 1990s, been giving out planning permissions so that property developers can make money without profit-sharing or social housing pay back – and sometimes at the cost of population clearances – let alone providing social infrastructure like schools or parks.

The form of property-led regeneration varies in different cities according to topography, demography and relation to the hinterland: it is central flats for the rich in London; middle-class homes inside the belt way in Amsterdam and in Rome; one and two-bedroom flats for young service-sector workers in Manchester. Here, the developers have built a private new town of lift-served apartments in the centre, where 50,000 young workers can sleep over (Folkman et al. 2016).

Why have states – central, regional or local – been so weak in the face of powerful corporate interests, especially in the classic foundational areas of land-use management and creation of transport infrastructures? Surely an important part of the answer is the widespread weakness of independent intermediary

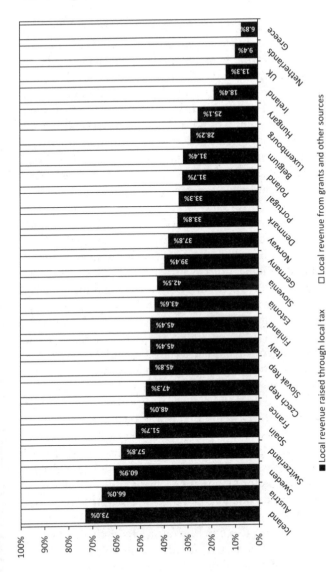

Exhibit 5.3 Local revenue raised through local taxes, 2012

Source: OECD Fiscal Decentralisation Database. www.oecd.org/tax/fiscal-decentralisation-database.htm

institutions between state and market. This problem has its origins in the post-war settlement, where intermediary institutions ended up playing a much smaller role than its liberal collectivist architects envisaged. Keynes (1926) favoured making port authorities or universities into 'semi-autonomous bodies within the State ... whose criterion of action within their own field is solely the public good as they understand it'. And, later, Beveridge (1948) argued that providential provision above the state insurance minimum could and would be made through 'friendly societies' or member-owned savings clubs, which were 'a democratic movement of mutual aid'.

But political control and practicalities intervened. The post-1945 Labour reforms in the UK reinforced central state power, which effectively weakened intermediary institutions. Furthermore, the British Treasury as finance ministry wanted to control budget allocations as its source of power. Thus the autonomous University Grants Committee, making funding allocations to individual universities for five-year periods, was replaced in 1989 by a funding committee answerable to Parliament via a minister. By the 2000s, the Arts Council was the one Keynesian intermediary that survived in the UK. Beveridge's friendly societies were completely beaten by large employer-based occupational pension schemes. The practical convenience of semi-automatic deductions from wages at source trumped the social attractions of club night in a local hall.

After the 1970s, a retreating state everywhere delegated more to third sector organisations but on terms and conditions which limited their independence. Given the bewildering diversity of third sector organisations (great and small charities, mutuals, religious foundations and other not-for-profit organisations) it is difficult to measure this. However, a comprehensive English study of third sector organisations with incomes of more than £100,000 in 2010 found that more than one half received state funding and between one quarter and one third of these organisations considered it their most important source of funding (Clifford, Rajme and Mohan 2010). The effects of financial dependence were reinforced by the state. As Scott (1998) has argued, the modern state is defined by its pursuit of synoptic legibility, whose form shifted in the 1990s with the emergence of the audit culture described by Power (1997), which burdened already financially dependent third sector organisations with new performance indicators.

The way things are now is neither natural nor inevitable, but it is the result of a trajectory which has created hard-to-shift conditions. In this right mess we cannot presume that any one actor can carry the burden of foundational initiative and leadership. Hence the need for hybrid organisations and foundational alliances where either local/regional government or intermediary institutions could take the leading role in pressing public policy for foundational renewal. As for the central state, it has at times tried to do too much for (and to) citizens, latterly as a kind of contract manager purchasing agreed outcomes; it might be much better for the central state to concentrate on facilitating experiment by coalitions of local and regional actors.

The four shifts outlined here are a mix of the utopian and the immediately practical – in other words they are entirely characteristic of any radical programme. Some, such as reconfiguration of the taxation system, could be implemented more or less immediately, if a political coalition could be created to support change. Others, such as the reconstruction of intermediary institutions, demand decades-long fostering because this requires cultural shifts as well as structural change, when citizens will only slowly see problems as theirs to solve. But the four are a package – they tell us what needs to change, and how, and thus they connect the visionary with the everyday.

But there is also another way of connecting the visionary with the everyday. The journey to a new political and economic practice does not have to wait upon some perfect alignment of conditions. We do not have to wait or ask permission to start with local experiments; many are already underway. The question is not just how to scale up but also how to promote political mobilisation which can shift conditions and constraints. And that is the lesson of the next section.

Starting out on foundational experiment

If the aim is to 'make hope possible', foundational experiment is an attractive idea because policy should aim for results and involve learning. We would all like to be pragmatists, and nobody wants to repeat mistakes. But policy experiment means quite different things for different people, and a key source of difference is whether it supports or disrupts the political status quo and established power. Here, foundational thinking aligns with the social innovation advocates of experiment like Roberto Unger rather than the 'what works' advocates like Charles Sabel.

In Charles Sabel and Jonathan Zeitlin's (2012) conceptualisation, 'experimentalist governance' is, in the spirit of John Dewey, a way of finding out what works in volatile and complex environments (see also Dorf and Sabel 1998). But this pragmatism is harnessed to conservative political ends, so that the apparatus of political power can negotiate the world more intelligently through a process of provisional setting and revision of policy objectives and instruments with central support for local discretion. Thus Sabel and Zeitlin praise what the EU is already doing across a broad array of policy domains like food and drug safety or environmental protection, and what national governments are already doing to improve schools.

In Roberto Unger's (2015) more radical conceptualisation, experiment becomes social innovation, designed to address unresolved problems which neither state nor market can solve, and which are beyond the standard remedies of progressive liberals and leftist social democrats. Furthermore, new ways of reorganising production and power can come out of 'small scale experiments' that develop into consequential alternatives.

'Maximalist' initiatives and experiments should be transforma-
tive, as they begin to engage state power and foreshadow not
a single programme but a new direction for society.

If the foundational aim is to realise something like Unger's
maximalist social innovation, the starting point in most cases
would be local and regional experiments. Innovative policy
can most easily break with the generic agenda of policymaking
elites after identifying the foundational needs of a specific
population and building on local assets. Those needs and
assets will vary by city and region. Hence, for example, on
transport, the need for surveys and focus groups to figure out
whether public transport is a high priority; and, if so, determin-
ing whether fares, timetable and investment can be influenced.
Furthermore, radical change is only likely to come through a
new politics of foundational alliance involving hybrid organisations with regional/local government, intermediary organisations and business working together. Such alliances are easiest
to put together on a local basis that would need to take
account of the variable capabilities and ambitions of voluntary
organisations and business.

The process of experiment should be one of making the
foundational visible, debatable and actionable. This requires
a basis of civic knowledge about the available foundational
goods and services. Service output, quality, innovation, financial
extraction and exploitation, organisational capabilities and
citizen participation all need to be taken into account. That
means recognising the supply-and-demand side of the foundational before reflecting on different orders of worth, and
then putting together a political alliance to change things.

This kind of foundational politics could be done in a variety
of ways. It allows for flexibility in motivation or instrument:
the sustaining political ideology could be liberal, socialist or
green of various hues, either solely or in some kind of combination. The only precondition is that the sponsors of foundational
experiment must recognise the widespread, albeit declining,
social consensus about the need for collectively funded and

organised foundational provision, and reject elite attempts to delegitimate this by invoking arguments about 'customers' and 'choice'. Thus foundational experiment does not mean working from a template of objectives, set actions and a preferred list of policy instruments. These can and should vary according to sponsor and circumstances.

Every experiment should be a pragmatic intervention to address the system problems of material and providential life. In doing this, experiments would seek to build on the asset base which is there in every European locality, including those labelled as deficient by standards of GVA or GDP. This asset base might include all or any of the following.

- The human competence and potential of those employed in producing foundational goods and services, presently often employed unconstructively in a variety of extractive and exploitative business models.
- A large controllable spend: not just government expenditure on providential services, but the everyday household spend on material requirements through utilities and groceries.
- A large stock of foundational capital, including public and private housing stock and material infrastructure in water, rail and electricity distribution.
- A distributed network of economically and socially capable productive firms and organisations: schools and hospitals, small business and micro firms (leaving aside the presently dysfunctional big corporates who dominate outsourcing).

This kind of experiment does not mean backing 'bottom-up' against 'top-down'. Turning local experiments into significant, scalable progress will only come from co-operation between many levels. As we have already argued, regional and national authorities with larger territories are required to press policies of social licensing; a municipality cannot stand up to a national supermarket chain or a multi-national like Amazon. Above all, foundational experiment needs a new and different kind of central state – a nation state which does not add constrain by prescribing metrics and outcomes but facilitates and enables change by creating frameworks within which foundational experiment can take place. Though this is not yet a coherent philosophy of central state action, there are already some examples of successful central facilitation intersecting with local agitation.

The re-municipalisation of water in France now takes place within a centrally created framework. After more than a decade of campaigning led by the French Green Party, central government, with all-party support, passed a new law in 2010 which enables two or more communes or municipalities to create a 'local public company' without the need to invite tenders from private companies (Hall, Lobina and Terhorst 2013, p. 200). In Germany, by the early 2010s, there were local campaigns and referenda plans for re-municipalisation of water in major cities such as Hamburg, Stuttgart, Bielefeld, Bremen, Frankfurt and Berlin (Hall, Lobina and Terhorst 2013, p. 303).

Under these conditions, foundational renewal can gather momentum and scale. Worldwide, since 2000 there have been 180 water re-municipalisations; since 2010, 33 of these have been in France, including the re-municipalisation of Paris water (Lobina, Kishimoto and Petitjean 2014). If such developments gather pace, they will begin to raise further issues. After all, transfer of ownership and operation to a not-for-profit is not in itself a guarantee of a successful foundational experiment. So here is a checklist of questions about what new interventions for foundational renewal could do; the questions could also form a basis for evaluating what they have done.

✓ Has foundational renewal *improved access to systems and services which matter to citizens locally*, and what is the changing balance between service quantity and quality?
✓ Has foundational renewal *displaced GDP or GVA with locally relevant targets* for making citizens' lives better: for instance, for houses with added energy efficient insulation?

✓ Has foundational renewal reduced labour exploitation and *delivered better jobs*? In other words, not only higher wages but changed roles by recomposing tasks and adding career progression.

✓ Has foundational renewal built *grounded firms with capability*? Can it accommodate the diversity of such firms and organisations, ranging from hospitals and retail chains to SMEs and micro firms?

✓ Has foundational renewal *redirected controllable public spend*? And done it not just for value for money or local spend but by building securely grounded SMEs.

✓ Has foundational renewal *raised the social ask* of privately owned utilities and supermarkets (as well as anchor institutions)? The critical issue here is: does the social licence require enterprises to put something back in return for their access to the expenditures of local households?

✓ Has foundational renewal *blocked extraction for capital* by evicting high return business models?

✓ Has foundational renewal *levered foundational assets* so that we get a social return? For instance, has it created community hubs by building specialist accommodation and re-using surplus shop/retail space?

These are modest tests which can be applied in a wide variety of different territorial settings. If there was progress by some of these criteria, experiments would be making the world a better place, not just by fixing the economy but also by inventing a more active citizenship. These tests deliberately depart from the idea of a template for and exemplar of reform as used by earlier generations of reformists on left and right in the 1980s and 1990s. These reformers were often motivated by the shining example of another country which supposedly did it better, reaped the benefits and therefore represented a better capitalist system and model for emulation. Thus Sweden was the exemplar of social democracy for the non-Nordic centre left; Germany with its Doktor-Ingenieur and its vocational training was the epitome of productionist technik for Anglo-Saxon critics of financialised capitalism; the deregulated post-1979 UK was the model of success for centrist reformers in countries like Italy and France lamenting the blockage of structural reform. As national exemplars get harder to find, we have the promotion of local exemplars like 'the Preston model' in the UK.[13]

But this exemplar approach is naïve and often leads to disillusion. It is naïve because the politics of becoming somewhere else is utopian; local specifics are always different, so the same causes will always have different effects. Learning from others is not the same as copying others; in any case, mimesis is impossible when historical conditions and pathways are different. It also leads to disillusion if the exemplar is idealised. The danger now is not gross deception of the kind involved in the Webbs' presentation of Stalin's Russia as a 'new civilisation', but the hyping of meagre local achievements for audiences who are eager to believe.

Having said this, we can still find inspirational historical cases: Vienna before 1934 and Bologna in the 1970s are striking examples where foundational priorities on housing and welfare were pressed in a transformational way in combination with an emphasis on democratic participation. In Vienna, under the social democrats between 1918 and 1934, the municipality built 60,000 flats as low-rent housing, delivered affordable gas and electricity and organised an infrastructure of kindergarten, schools and health clinics. In Bologna in the 1970s under the PCI, the municipality delivered fare-free buses, more preventive medicine and housing co-ops (Jäggi, Müller and Schmid 1977).

Bologna remains an inspiration as an experiment in inserting alternative principles and practice or 'elements of revolution' into capitalist host bodies which would ordinarily reject them. Red Vienna was described by an American observer as 'probably the most successful municipality in the world' (Gunther 1940, p. 315), just as Bologna's political practice was praised by a British leftist in the late 1970s as different from the parliamentary Labour pitch of 'vote Labour and we will do this for you' (Green 1978). Nevertheless, Vienna and Bologna cannot be any kind of model because their successes and failures were of their time and place. But precisely because of this, they can give us grounds for optimism. We cannot, and would not want to, recreate the institutional and political conditions that sustained 'Red Vienna' and proletarian Bologna. But we are the heirs of conditions that simply could not exist in these historical exemplars.

The range of progressive alliances are unimaginably wider now than was conceivable in the Vienna of the 1920s or Bologna of the 1970s: alliances of traditional male-dominated groups of workers and intellectuals have given way to a spectrum that encompasses advocates for ethnic minority, gender, LGBT and disability rights. Moreover, there is a more straightforward difference that should give us grounds for optimism: our societies, for all the destruction of the great financial crisis, are much wealthier than in the past. Many things stand in the way of recreating a foundational economy that fosters human capability and flourishing. Scarcity of resource is not one of them. As Europeans, why not start out now on foundational renewal, rediscover an experimental tradition and reinvent radical political practice in a way that cannot be extinguished.

Notes

1 GDP is measured as the value of all the finished goods and services produced in a particular place (e.g. a region or nation) during a specific period (e.g. a year); GVA (Gross Value Added) is measured as the value of goods and services produced (in a particular place during a specific period), minus the cost of all inputs and raw materials that are directly attributable to its production.

2   See: BIEN Current Basic Income Experiments http://basicincome.
    org/news/2017/05/basic-income-experiments-and-those-so-called-
    early-2017-updates/ (accessed 8 February 2018).

3   See, for example, Unger's interview published by the Institute
    for Public Policy Research in Unger and Wood (2014).

4   Source: https://corporate.ryanair.com/about-us/fact-and-figures/
    (accessed 8 February 2018).

5   There are examples of successful transformations with significant
    public health benefits: most notably work in the 1970s in North
    Karelia, Finland (Buettner 2015).

6   Source: www.evgoh.com/2017/07/19/cleveland-people-brett-jones-
    president-evergreen-energy-solutions-cleveland-scene-magazine/
    (accessed 8 February 2018).

7   Source: https://fullfact.org/health/spending-english-nhs/ (accessed
    8 February 2018).

8   Source: https://taxfoundation.org/corporate-income-tax-rates-
    around-world-2015/ (accessed 8 February 2018).

9   See, for example, *The Economist* blog at: https://www.economist.
    com/blogs/economist-explains/2014/11/economist-explains-0
    (accessed 8 February 2018); and the Institute of Economic Affairs
    at: https://iea.org.uk/blog/the-case-for-a-land-value-tax-0 (accessed
    8 February 2018).

10 See: https://euobserver.com/social/139922 (accessed 8 Febru-
    ary 2018); https://iea.org.uk/blog/the-case-for-a-land-value-tax
    (accessed 8 February 2018).

11 For example, according to the UK Government 'Smart Specialisa-
    tion in England is an approach to investment in innovation which
    … applies to innovation in the fields of technology, business
    processes, agricultural industries and social innovation, including
    the reform of public services' (Department for Business Innovation
    and Skills 2015, p. 4).

12 https://ec.europa.eu/commission/news/smart-specialisation-
    european-regions-2017-jul-18_en (accessed 8 February 2018).

13 See: https://thenextsystem.org/the-preston-model (accessed 8
    February 2018).

Measuring and shaping the economy: afterword by Andy Haldane

In most natural sciences, the units of measurement are well-established and near-universally agreed upon, either by law or convention. For mass, it is kilograms; for time, seconds; for distance, light years from Earth etc. We even have a sub-science – metrology – tasked with arriving at these standards. These units of measurement allow us to quantify objectively natural phenomenon. They are a core building block of models of behaviour in (physical, chemical or biological) systems and provide a means of evaluating policies which reshape these systems. In this role, units of measurement have been fundamental to scientific, and indeed societal, advance.

When we turn to the social sciences, the units of measurement are less well-established and understood. There are rarely unified laws or agreed conventions. Instead there is custom and practice. This does not make the chosen units of measurement good or bad, right or wrong. But it does make them a point of debate and, sometimes, a bone of contention. This fascinating book, *Foundational economy*, can be seen as a contribution to this debate about measuring, understanding and, ultimately, reshaping economic systems. More than that, it is a critique of existing custom and practice when measuring, understanding and shaping the economy. This critique is as foundational as the book's title.

This critique goes to a set of deep questions in economics and economic policy. How do we assess how well society is being served by the economy? The existing convention, based around individuals' consumption of private goods – in short, GDP? Or an alternative, based on everyone having sufficient access to social, as well as private, goods – a broader measure of well-being?

Where should we focus when measuring the societal contribution of different sectors? The private sector, as is the convention, the single largest contributor to value-added in the economy? Or a blend of the private, public and third sectors, each of whom contributes to the creation of social goods, such as infrastructure, education, training and banking.

Which set of policy interventions are best-suited to creating the goods and services, individual and social, that people require? One based on the twin pillars of monetary and fiscal policy, on which so much weight has been placed over recent years? Or one that augments these levers with structural policies to support provision of the social goods and services essential to everyone?

The contours of this policy debate have already changed over recent years. Internationally, there is greater recognition than there has been for a generation on the importance of structural policy intervention to support provision of essential services, from transport to education to banking. As one example, the UK government has begun to sketch the contours of an 'industrial strategy'. This speaks to a number of the issues put centre-stage in *Foundational Economy*. For example, the spatial or geographic dimension of policy is growing in public policy importance. So too is the need for institutions that create all-important civic goods, such as schools, transport and training.

It is early days for industrial strategies and even earlier ones for foundational economies. We are some way short of well-defined and widely-agreed set of new weights and measures for the economy. And we are a long way short of knowing which policy tools best deliver the private and collective goods society needs to flourish. This book tackles head-on some of those big questions about the economy. It also begins the process of providing answers. As in the natural sciences, as an approach I think this offers hope for societal, as well as scientific, advance.

Andy Haldane

References

ABC News (2017) 'South-Australian-blackouts-costing-businesses-money/'. At: www.abc.net.au/news/2016-12-09/sa-blackout-costs-could-have-been-worse-business-sa-says/8106600 (accessed 8 February 2018).

Amsden, A.H. (1989) *Asia's Next Giant: South Korea and Late Industrialization.* Oxford: Oxford University Press.

Atkinson, A.B. (2015) *Inequality: What Can Be Done?* Cambridge MA: Harvard University Press.

Bartik, T.J. and Erickcek, G. (2008) 'The local economy impact of "eds & meds"'. Brookings Metropolitan Policy Programme. At: https://www.brookings.edu/wp-content/uploads/2016/06/metropolitan_economies_report.pdf (accessed 8 February 2018).

Bayliss, K. and Hall, D. (2017) *Bringing Water into Public Ownership: Costs and Benefits.* London. At: http://gala.gre.ac.uk/17277/10/17277%20HALL_Bringing_Water_into_Public_Ownership_%28Rev%27d%29_2017.pdf (accessed 8 February 2018).

Bentham, J., Bowman, A., Froud, J., Johal, S., Leaver, A. and Williams, K. (2013) *Against New Industrial Strategy: Framing, Motifs and Absences.* Manchester and Milton Keynes: Centre for Research on Socio-Cultural Change University of Manchester. At: https://foundationaleconomycom.files.wordpress.com/2017/01/wp126.pdf (accessed 8 February 2018).

Berle, A. (1962) 'A new look at management responsibility'. Lecture to the Bureau of Industrial Relations, University of Michigan, 9 April 1962. At: http://3197d6d14b5f19f2f440-5e13d29c4c016cf96cbbfd197c579b45.r81.cf1.rackcdn.com/collection/

papers/1960/1962_0409_ManagementBerleT.pdf (accessed 8 February 2018).

Beveridge, W. (1948) *Voluntary Action: A Report on Methods of Social Advance*. New York: Macmillan.

Boltanski, L. and Thévenot, L. (2006) [1991] *On Justification: The Economies of Worth*. Princeton: Princeton University Press.

Born, B. and Purcell, M. (2006) 'Avoiding the local trap: scale and food systems in planning research', Journal of Planning Education and Research 26, 195–207.

Bowman, A., Folkman, P., Froud, J., Johal, S., Law, J., Leaver, A., Moran, M. and Williams, K. (2013a) *The Great Train Robbery: The Economic and Political Consequences of Rail Privatisation*. Manchester and Milton Keynes: Centre for Research on Socio-Cultural Change. At: https://foundationaleconomycom.files.wordpress.com/2017/01/the-great-train-robbery.pdf (accessed 8 February 2018).

Bowman, A., Folkman, P., Froud, J., Johal, S., Law, J., Leaver, A., Moran, M. and Williams, K. (2013b) *The Conceit of Enterprise: Train Operators and Trade Narrative. CRESC Response to ATOC's 'Growth and Prosperity Report'*. Manchester and Milton Keynes: Centre for Research on Socio-Cultural Change. At: https://foundationaleconomycom.files.wordpress.com/2017/01/the-conceit-of-enterprise.pdf (accessed 8 February 2018).

Bowman, A., Ertürk, I., Froud, J., Johal, S., Law, J., Leaver, A., Moran, M. and Williams, K. (2014) *The End of the Experiment: From Competition to the Foundational Economy*. Manchester: Manchester University Press.

Bowman, A. Ertürk, I., Folkman, P., Froud, J., Haslam, C., Sukhdev, J., Leaver, A., Moran, M., Tsitsianis, N. and Williams, K. (2015) *What a Waste: Outsourcing and How it Goes Wrong*. Manchester: Manchester University Press.

Braudel, F. (1981) *The Structures of Everyday Life: Civilization and Capitalism. Volume I*. (Tr: Sîan Renolds). New York: Harper and Row.

Brill, L. Cowie, L., Folkman, P., Froud, J., Johal, S., Leaver, A., Moran, M. and Williams, K. (2015) *What Wales Could Be*. Report for FSB Wales. Manchester and Milton Keynes: Centre for Research on Socio-Cultural Change. At: https://

foundationaleconomycom.files.wordpress.com/2017/01/what-wales-could-be.pdf (accessed 8 February 2018).

Brynjolfsen, E. and McAfee, A. (2012) *Race Against the Machine*. Lexington, MA: Digital Frontier Press.

Buettner, D. (2015) The Finnish town that went on a diet, *The Atlantic*, 7 April 2015. At: https://www.theatlantic.com/health/archive/2015/04/finlands-radical-heart-health-transformation/389766/ (accessed 8 February 2018).

Burns, D., Cowie, L., Earle, J., Folkman, P., Froud, J., Hyde, P., Johal, S., Jones, I.R., Killett, A. and Williams, K. (2016) *Where Does the Money Go? Financialised Chains and the Crisis in Residential Care*. Manchester and Milton Keynes: Centre for Research on Socio-Cultural Change. At: https://foundationaleconomycom.files.wordpress.com/2017/01/wheredoesthemoneygo.pdf (accessed 8 February 2018).

CAFOD (2014) *What is Inclusive Growth?* CAFOD discussion paper, August 2014. At: https://cafod.org.uk/content/download/17223/133621/file/Inclusive%20Growth%20full%20paper.pdf (accessed 8 February 2018).

Chazan, G. (2017) 'Cracks appear in Germany's cash-starved infrastructure', *Financial Times*, 4 August 2017.

Christophers, B. (2011) 'Making finance productive', Economy and Society, 40:1, 112–40.

Cicchetti, A. and Gasbarrini, A. (2016) 'The healthcare service in Italy: regional variability'. At: www.europeanreview.org/wp/wp-content/uploads/The-healthcare-service-in-Italy-regional-variability.pdf (accessed 8 February 2018).

Clifford, C. (2016) 'Elon Musk: Robots will take your jobs, government will have to pay your wage'. CNBC, 4 November 2016. At: https://www.cnbc.com/2016/11/04/elon-musk-robots-will-take-your-jobs-government-will-have-to-pay-your-wage.html (accessed 8 February 2018).

Clifford, D., Rajme, F.G. and Mohan, J. (2010) 'How dependent is the third sector on public funding? Evidence from the National Survey of Third Sector Organisation'. Birmingham: Third Sector Research Centre, Working Paper 45. At: www.birmingham.ac.uk/generic/tsrc/documents/tsrc/working-papers/working-paper-45.pdf (accessed 8 February 2018).

Cohn, G. (1910) 'Municipal socialism', The Economic Journal, 20: 561–8.

Committee on Standards in Public Life (2014) 'Ethical standards for providers of public services, June 2014'. At: https://www.gov.uk/government/uploads/system/uploads/attachment_data/file/336942/CSPL_EthicalStandards_web.pdf (accessed 8 February 2018).

Committee on Standards in Public Life (2015) 'Ethical standards for providers of public services – guidance, December 2015'. At: https://www.gov.uk/government/uploads/system/uploads/attachment_data/file/481535/6.1291_CO_LAL_Ethical_standards_of_public_life_report_Interactive__2_.pdf (accessed 8 February 2018).

Coyle, D. (2014) GDP: A Brief But Affectionate History. Princeton: Princeton University Press.

Crouch, C. (2009). 'Privatised Keynesianism: an unacknowledged policy regime', British Journal of Politics and International Relations, 11:3, 382–99.

Cutler T., Williams K. and Williams J. (1986) Keynes, Beveridge and Beyond. London: Routledge and Kegan Paul

Deaton, A. (2014) The Great Escape: Health, Wealth, and the Origins of Inequality. Princeton: Princeton University Press.

Deb, S. (2015) 'Gap between GDP and HDI: are the rich country experiences different from the poor?' IARIW-OECD Special Conference: W(h)ither the SNA? Paris. At: http://iariw.org/papers/2015/deb.pdf (accessed 8 February 2018).

Department for Business Innovation and Skills (2015) Smart Specialisation in England. Submission to the European Commission. London: BIS.

Dorf, M.C. and Sabel, C.F. (1998) 'A constitution of democratic experimentalism'. Cornell Law Faculty Publications, Paper 120. At: http://scholarship.law.cornell.edu/facpub/120 (accessed 8 February 2018).

Earle, J., Moran, C., and Ward-Perkins, Z. (2017) The Econocracy: The Perils of Leaving Economics to the Experts. Manchester: Manchester University Press.

Earle, J., Froud, J., Haslam, C., Johal, S., Moran, M. and Williams, K. (2017) What Wales Can Do: Asset Based Policies and the Foundational Economy. CREW/University of Manchester. At: https://foundationaleconomy.com/2017/06/23/what-wales-can-do-asset-based-policies-and-the-foundational-economy/ (accessed 8 February 2018).

Edgerton, D. (2008) *The Shock of the Old: Technology and Global History Since 1900*. London: Profile.

Elliott, J. and Kanagasooriam, J. (2017) *Public Opinion in the Post-Brexit Era: Economic Attitudes in Modern Britain'*. London: Legatum Institute. At: https://www.li.com/activities/publications/public-opinion-in-the-post-brexit-era-economic-attitudes-in-modern-britain (accessed 8 February 2018).

Esping Andersen, G. (1990) *The Three Worlds of Welfare Capitalism*. Princeton: Princeton University Press.

European Environment Agency (2017) *Air Quality in Europe 2017*. EEA Report 13/2017. Luxembourg: Publications Office of the EU. At: https://www.eea.europa.eu/publications/air-quality-in-europe-2017 (accessed 8 February 2018).

Evans, R. (1987) *Death in Hamburg: Society and Politics in the Cholera Years 1830–1910*. Oxford: Oxford University Press.

Fioramonti, L. (2013) *Gross Domestic Problem: The Politics Behind the World's Most Powerful Number*. London: Zed Books

Fioramonti, L. (2017) *The World After GDP: Politics, Business and Society in the Post-Growth Era*. Cambridge: Polity.

Florio, M. (2013) 'Rethinking on public enterprise: editorial introduction and some personal remarks on the research agenda', International Review of Applied Economics, 27:2, 135–49.

Folkman, P., Froud, J., Johal, S., Tomaney, J. and Williams, K. (2016) *Manchester Transformed: Why we Need a Reset of City Region Policy*. Manchester and Milton Keynes: Centre for Research on Socio-Cultural Change. At: https://foundationaleconomycom.files.wordpress.com/2017/01/manchestertransformed.pdf (accessed 8 February 2018).

Frey, C. and Osborne, M. (2013) 'The future of employment: how susceptible are jobs to computerisation?' Oxford: Oxford Martin School. At: https://www.oxfordmartin.ox.ac.uk/downloads/academic/The_Future_of_Employment.pdf (accessed 8 February 2018).

Froud, J., Johal, S., Leaver, A. and Williams, K. (2006) *Financialization and Strategy: Narrative and Numbers*. London: Routledge.

Froud, J., Hayes, S., Wei, H. and Williams, K. (2017) *Coming Back? Capability and Precarity in UK Textiles and Apparel*. Manchester:

University of Manchester. At: https://foundationaleconomycom. files.wordpress.com/2017/02/coming-back-capability-and-precarity-in-uk-textiles-and-apparel-march-2017.pdf (accessed 8 February 2018).

Galbraith, J.K. (1958) *The Affluent Society*. New York: Houghton Mifflin.

Gamble, A. and Kelly, G. (2001) 'Shareholder value and the stakeholder debate in the UK', Corporate Governance, 9:2, 110–17.

Gordon, R. (2016) *The Rise and Fall of American Growth: The U.S. Standard of Living since the Civil War*. Princeton: Princeton University Press.

GMCA (2013) *Stronger Together: Greater Manchester Strategy*. Manchester: Greater Manchester Combined Authority. At: https://www.greatermanchester-ca.gov.uk/downloads/file/8/stronger_together_-_greater_manchester_strategy (accessed 8 February 2018).

GMCA (2016) *Draft Greater Manchester Spatial Framework*. Manchester: Greater Manchester Combined Authority. At: https://www.greatermanchester-ca.gov.uk/downloads/file/371/draft_greater_manchester_spatial_framework_-_full_version (accessed 8 February 2018).

Green, D. (1978) 'What does Red Bologna mean for Britain?' *Marxism Today, June 1978*, pp. 195–8.

Green, T.H. (1895/1941) *Lectures on the Principles of Political Obligation*. With Preface by B. Bosanquet, and Introduction by A.D. Lindsay. London: Longmans.

Grout, P., Jenkins, A. and Zalewska, A. (2001) 'Privatisation of utilities and the asset value problem'. University of Bristol: CMPO Working Paper Series No. 01/412. At: http://citeseerx.ist.psu.edu/viewdoc/download?doi=10.1.1.147.9211&rep=rep1&type=pdf (accessed 8 February 2018).

Gunther, J. (1940) *Inside Europe*. New York: Harper & Brothers.

Hall, D., Lobina, E. and Terhorst, P. (2013) 'Remunicipalisation in the early twenty-first century'. International Review of Applied Economics, 27: 2, 193–214.

Hammer, N. (2015) *New Industry on a Skewed Playing Field: Supply Chain Relations and Working Conditions in UK Garment Manufacturing*: Leicester: University of Leicester Centre for Sustainable Work and Employment Futures. At: https://lra.le.ac.uk/

bitstream/2381/36497/2/Hammer%20etal%202015%20ETI%20
Report.pdf (accessed 8 February 2018).

Harford, T. (2011) 'You're wrong – we're all wealth creators' *Financial Times*, 2 December 2011.

Hill, C. (1961) *Century of Revolution*. New York: Norton.

Industrial Strategy Commission (2017) *The Final Report of the Industrial Strategy Commission*. Universities of Manchester and Sheffield. At: http://industrialstrategycommission.org.uk/wp-content/uploads/2017/10/The-Final-Report-of-the-Industrial-Strategy-Commission.pdf (accessed 8 February 2018).

Jacobs, J. (1961) *The Death and Life of Great American Cities*. Boston: Random House

Jäggi, M., Müller, R. and Schmid, S. (1977) *Red Bologna*. Worthing: Littlehampton Book Services Ltd.

Johal, S. and Williams, K. (2013) 'The Enfield experiment'. At: http://hummedia.manchester.ac.uk/institutes/cresc/sites/default/files/EnfieldExperiment_0.pdf (accessed 8 February 2018).

Johal, S., Moran, M. and Williams, K. (2016) 'Breaking the constitutional silence: the public services industry and government'. The Political Quarterly, 87:3, 390–7.

Jutti, P.S. and Katko, T.S. (Eds) (2005) *Water, Time and European Cities: History Matters for the Futures*, Tampere: Tampere University Press.

Kahneman, D. and Tversky, A. (1979) 'Prospect theory: an analysis of decision under risk', Econometrica, 47:2, 263–92.

Kay, J. (2017) 'The basics of basic income', Intereconomics, 52:2, 69–74.

Keynes, J.M. (1926) *The End of Laissez Faire*. London: Royal Economic Society.

Kuznets, S. (1934) *National Income, 1929–32*. New York: National Bureau of Economic Research, Bulletin 49, 7 June, pp. 1–13. At: www.nber.org/chapters/c2258.pdf (accessed 8 February 2018).

Legambiente (2014), *Rapporto Pendolaria 2014. La situazione e gli scenari del trasporto ferroviario pendolare in Italia*, Roma. At: https://www.legambiente.it/pendolaria-2014 (accessed 8 February 2018).

Lenger, F. (2012) *European Cities in the Modern Era 1850–1914*. Brill: Leiden.

Littlechild, S. (1983) *Regulation of British Telecommunications' Profitability*. London: Department of Industry.

Littlechild, S. (1986) *Economic Regulation of Privatised Water Authorities*. London: Her Majesty's Stationery Office.

Lobina, E. and Hall, D. (2001) *UK Water Privatisation: A Briefing*. London: Public Services International Research Unit.

Lobina, E., Kishimoto, S. and Petitjean, O. (2014) *Here to Stay: Water Remuncipalisation as a Global Trend*. London: Public Services International Research Unit. At: www.psiru.org/sites/default/files/2014-11-W-HeretoStay.pdf (accessed 8 February 2018).

Lockwood, D. (1996) 'Civic integration and class formation', British Journal of Sociology 47:3, 531–50.

Lyson, T. (2006) 'Big business and community welfare: revisiting a classic study by C. Wright Mills and Melville Ulmer. American Journal of Economics and Sociology 65(5):1001–1024.

Marshall, T.H. (1950) *Citizenship and Social Class and Other Essays*. Cambridge: Cambridge University Press.

Martin, C., Pawson, H. and van den Nouwelant, R. (2016) 'Housing policy and the housing system in Australia: an overview. Report for the Shaping Housing Futures Project'. Sydney: City Futures Research Centre, University of New South Wales. At: http://shapingfutures.gla.ac.uk/wp-content/uploads/2016/09/Shaping-Housing-Futures-Australia-background-paper.pdf (accessed 8 February 2018).

Mazzucato, M. (2015) *The Entrepreneurial State: Debunking Public vs. Private Sector Myths*. London: Anthem Press.

McColvin, G.B. (2012) *Louis XIV's Assault on Privilege*. Mount Hope: University of Rochester.

McKinsey Global Institute (2017) *A Future That Works: Automation, Employment and Productivity*. McKinsey Global Institute.

Miles, I., Kastrinos, N., Bilderbeek, R., den Hertog, P., Flanagan,K., Huntink, W. and Bouman, M. (1995) *Knowledge-intensive business services: users, carriers and sources of innovation*. Manchester: PREST. At: https://www.research.manchester.ac.uk/portal/files/32800224/FULL_TEXT.PDF (accessed 8 February 2018).

Mills, C.W., and Ulmer, M. (1946) *Small Business and Civic Welfare: Report of the Smaller War Plants Corporation to the Special Committee to Study Problems of American Small Business*,

Document135, U.S. Senate, 79th Congress, 2nd session, Feb 13, Washington, D.C. US Govt Printing Office.

Milne, R. (2016) 'Swedish angst grows over tensions in public-private model'. *Financial Times*, 16 October 2016.

Mitchell, B., Chambers, D. and Crafts, N. (2009) *How Good Was the Profitability Of British Railways, 1870–1912?* Warwick: University of Warwick Research Paper No. 859. At: https://warwick.ac.uk/fac/soc/economics/research/workingpapers/2008/twerp_859c.pdf (accessed 8 February 2018).

Moran, M. (2001) 'Not steering but drowning: policy catastrophes and the regulatory state'. Political Quarterly, 72:4, 414–27.

Morris, L. (2016) 'Squaring the circle: domestic welfare, migrant rights, and human rights', Citizenship Studies, 20:6–7, 693–709.

Nussbaum, M. (2000) *Women and Human Development: The Capabilities Approach*. Cambridge: Cambridge University Press.

OECD (2013) *Innovation-Driven Growth in Regions: The Role of Smart Specialisation*, Paris: OECD.

OECD (2014) *Report on the OECD Framework for Inclusive Growth*. Paris: OCED. At: https://www.oecd.org/mcm/IG_MCM_ENG.pdf (accessed 8 February 2018).

ONS (Office for National Statistics) (2017) 'Graduates in the UK Labour Market: 2017'. 24 November 2017. At: https://www.ons.gov.uk/employmentandlabourmarket/peopleinwork/employmentandemployeetypes/articles/graduatesintheuklabourmarket/2017 (accessed 8 February 2018).

Owen, J.R. and Kemp, D. (2013) 'Social licence and mining: a critical perspective', Resources Policy, 38:1, 29–35.

People's Plan Greater Manchester (2017) 'People's Plan Greater Manchester, April 2017'. At: www.peoplesplangm.org.uk/wp-content/uploads/2017/04/PEOPLES-PLAN-April-2017.pdf (accessed 8 February 2018).

Piketty, T. (2014) *Capital in the Twenty-First Century*. Cambridge MA: Harvard University Press.

Plank, L. (2016) 'Financializing German infrastructure: insurance companies and pension funds riding the austerity wave'. Paper presented at the Social Innovation Colloquium, University of Cardiff, May 2016.

Polanyi, K. (1944) *The Great Transformation*. New York: Farrar and Rinehart.

Power, M. (1997) *The Audit Society: Rituals of Verification*. Oxford: Oxford University Press.

Ramesh M., Aralal, E. and Wu, X. (2010) *Reasserting the Public in Public Services: New Public Management Reforms*. London: Routledge.

Raworth, K. (2017) *Doughnut Economics*. London: Random House.

Reich, R. (2015) 'Labor Day 2028'. Blog, 31 August 2015. At: http://robertreich.org/post/128058937635 (accessed 8 February 2018).

Rittel, H. and Webber, M. (1973) 'Dilemmas in a general theory of planning', Policy Sciences, 4:2, 155–69.

Ryan-Collins, J., Lloyd, T. and Macfarlane, L. (2017) *Rethinking the Economics of Land and Housing*. London: Zed Books.

Sabel, C. and Zeitlin, J. (2012) 'Experimentalist governance', in D. Levi-Faur (ed.), *The Oxford Handbook of Governance*. Oxford: Oxford University Press, pp. 169–83.

Sayer, A. (2000) 'Moral economy and political economy', Studies in Political Economy, 61:1, 79–104.

Sayer, A. (2011) *Why Things Matter to People*. Cambridge: Cambridge University Press.

Scott, J.C. (1998) *Seeing Like a State: How Certain Schemes to Improve the Human Condition Have Failed*. New Haven, CT: Yale University Press.

Sen, A. (1999) *Development as Freedom*. Oxford: Oxford University Press.

Sherib. G and Sorrer, S. (2017) 'Power cuts rattle Libyan government. 19 Jan 2017'. Bloomberg News. At: https://www.bloomberg.com/news/articles/2017-01-19 (accessed 8 February 2018).

Social Prosperity Network (2017) *Social Prosperity for the Future: A Proposal for Universal Basic Services*. London: University College London Institute for Global Prosperity. At: https://www.ucl.ac.uk/bartlett/igp/sites/bartlett/files/universal_basic_services_-_the_institute_for_global_prosperity_.pdf (accessed 8 February 2018).

Standing, G. (2017) *Basic Income and How We Can Make it Happen*. London: Pelican.

Stiglitz, J.E., Sen, A. and Fitoussi, J-P. (2009) *Report by the Commission on the Measurement of Economic Performance and Social Progress*. Brussels: European Commission. At: http://ec.europa.eu/eurostat/documents/118025/118123/Fitoussi+Commission+report (accessed 8 February 2018).

Streeck, W. (2015) *The Rise of the European Consolidation State*. Cologne: Max Planck Institute for the Study of Societies. Discussion paper 15/1. At: https://wolfgangstreeck.com/2015/02/13/the-rise-of-the-european-consolidation-state/ (accessed 8 February 2018).

Tawney, R.H. (1931) *Equality*. London: Allen and Unwin.

Thatcher, M. (1976) 'Speech at Annual Dinner Dance of the Finchley Conservative Association, 31 January'. www.margaretthatcher.org/document/102947 (accessed 8 February 2018).

Tilly, C. (1985) 'War making and state making as organized crime', in Davis, P., Rueschemeyer, D. and Skocpol, T. (eds), *Bringing the State Back In*. Cambridge: Cambridge University Press, pp. 169–86.

Titmuss, R.M. (1950) *Problems of Social Policy*. London: HMSO.

Titmuss, R.M. (1958) *Essays on the Welfare State*. London: Allen and Unwin.

UK Government (2017) 'PM unveils plans for a modern industrial strategy fit for global Britain'. Press release 22 January 2017. At: https://www.gov.uk/government/news/pm-unveils-plans-for-a-modern-industrial-strategy-fit-for-global-britain (accessed 8 February 2018).

Unger R.M. (2015) 'Conclusion: the task of the social innovation movement', in Nicholls A., Simon J. and Gabriel M. (eds), *New Frontiers in Social Innovation Research*. London: Palgrave Macmillan, pp. 233–51.

Unger, R.M. and Wood, S. (2014) 'Roberto Unger interview on the means and ends of the political left', *Juncture*, 22 January 2014. At: https://www.ippr.org/juncture/juncture-interview-roberto-unger-on-the-means-and-ends-of-the-political-left (accessed 8 February 2018).

Vatican Press Service (2017) 'Pastoral visit of the Holy Father Francis to the Archdiocese of Genoa (27 May 2017) – Meeting with the world of work at the Ilva Factory, 27.05.2017'. At: https://press.vatican.va/content/salastampa/en/bollettino/pubblico/2017/05/27/170527a.html (accessed 8 February 2018).

Wachman, R. (2011) 'Southern Cross's incurably flawed business model let down the vulnerable', *The Guardian*, 16 July 2011. At: https://www.theguardian.com/business/2011/jul/16/southern-cross-incurable-sick-business-model?INTCMP=ILCNETTXT3487 (accessed 8 February 2018).

Wade, R. (1990) *Governing the Market. Economic Theory and the Role of Government in East Asian Industrialization*. Princeton: Princeton University Press.

Waring, M. (1990) *If Women Counted: A New Feminist Economics*. San Francisco: Harper Collins.

Weale, A. (1991) 'Citizenship beyond borders', in Vogel, U. and Moran, M. (eds), *The Frontiers of Citizenship*. London: Macmillan, pp. 155–65.

Webster, C. (2002) *The National Health Service: A Political History*. Oxford: Oxford University Press.

Welsh Government (2017a) *Our Valleys, Our Future*. At: http://gov.wales/docs/dsjlg/publications/comm/170720-our-valleys-our-future-env2.pdf (accessed 8 February 2018).

Welsh Government (2017b) *Our Valleys, Our Future*. Evidence Paper. At: http://gov.wales/docs/dsjlg/publications/comm/170720-evidence-paper-en-v1.pdf (accessed 8 February 2018).

Welsh Government (2017c) *Our Valleys, Our Future*. Report of the Taskforce for the Valleys. At: http://gov.wales/topics/people-and-communities/communities/taskforce-for-the-valleys/?lang=en (accessed 8 February 2018).

Welsh Government (2017d) *Prosperity for All: Economic Action Plan*. At: http://gov.wales/topics/businessandeconomy/welsh-economy/economic-action-plan/?lang=en (accessed 8 February 2018).

Widerquist, K. (2013) *Independence, Propertylessness, and Basic Income: A Theory of Freedom as the Power to Say No*. London: Palgrave.

Williams, R. (1989) *Resources of Hope*. London: Verso.

Wollmann, H. (2016) 'Provision of public and social services in European countries: from public sector to marketization and reverse – or, what next?' in Kuhlmann, S. and Bouckaert, G. (eds), *Local Public Sector Reforms in Times of Crises; National Trajectories and International Comparisons*. London: Palgrave Macmillan, pp. 187–204.

Wright, L. and Besslich, N. (2017) 'What makes Britain's railways great?' Rail Delivery Group. At: https://www.raildeliverygroup.com/files/Publications/2017-06_what_makes_Britains_railways_great.pdf (accessed 8 February 2018).

Yeung, H.W-C. (2016) *Strategic Coupling: East Asian Industrial Transformation in the New Global Economy*. Ithaca: Cornell University Press.